Merrill, Cavafy,
Poems, and Dreams

POETS ON POETRY

David Lehman, General Editor
Donald Hall, Founding Editor

New titles

Tess Gallagher, *Soul Barnacles*
Rachel Hadas, *Merrill, Cavafy, Poems, and Dreams*
Ron Padgett, *The Straight Line*
Charles Simic, *A Fly in the Soup*

Recently published

Edward Hirsch, *Responsive Reading*
John Koethe, *Poetry at One Remove*
Yusef Komunyakaa, *Blue Notes*
Philip Larkin, *Required Writing*
Alicia Suskin Ostriker, *Dancing at the Devil's Party*
James Tate, *The Route as Briefed*

Also available are collections by

A. R. Ammons, Robert Bly, Philip Booth, Marianne Boruch,
Hayden Carruth, Fred Chappell, Amy Clampitt, Tom Clark,
Douglas Crase, Robert Creeley, Donald Davie, Peter Davison,
Tess Gallagher, Suzanne Gardinier, Allen Grossman, Thom Gunn,
John Haines, Donald Hall, Joy Harjo, Robert Hayden,
Daniel Hoffman, Jonathan Holden, John Hollander,
Andrew Hudgins, Josephine Jacobsen, Weldon Kees,
Galway Kinnell, Mary Kinzie, Kenneth Koch, Richard Kostelanetz,
Maxine Kumin, Martin Lammon (editor), David Lehman,
Philip Levine, John Logan, William Logan, William Matthews,
William Meredith, Jane Miller, Carol Muske, John Frederick Nims,
Geoffrey O'Brien, Gregory Orr, Marge Piercy, Anne Sexton,
Charles Simic, Louis Simpson, William Stafford, Anne Stevenson,
May Swenson, Richard Tillinghast, Diane Wakoski, C. K. Williams,
Alan Williamson, Charles Wright, and James Wright

Rachel Hadas

Merrill, Cavafy, Poems, and Dreams

Ann Arbor

THE UNIVERSITY OF MICHIGAN PRESS

Copyright by the University of Michigan 2000
All rights reserved
Published in the United States of America by
The University of Michigan Press
Manufactured in the United States of America
⊗ Printed on acid-free paper

2003   2002   2001   2000   4   3   2   1

A CIP catalog record for this book is available
from the British Library.

Library of Congress Cataloging-in-Publication Data

Hadas, Rachel.
    Merrill, Cavafy, poems, and dreams / Rachel Hadas.
        p. cm.
    Includes bibliographical references.
    ISBN 0-472-09719-9 (alk. paper)
    ISBN 0-472-06719-2 (pbk. : alk. paper)
    1. Hadas, Rachel—Authorship.   2. Merrill, James Ingram—
Criticism and interpretation.   3. American poetry—20th
century—History and criticism.   4. Greek poetry—History and
criticism.   5. Poetry.   I. Title.
PS3558.A3116 M47 2000
809.1—dc21   00-008597

Preface

This selection of my prose from the past twenty years is divided into four sections. The first includes some (by no means all) of the pieces I've written on Greek poets ranging from Homer to Karyotakis, in which I consider a new translation, a whole career, a single book, or a few poems. The second section includes some (again, not all) of what I've written about the late James Merrill. The third section, more miscellaneous, includes pieces on Alan Ansen, Mona Van Duyn, the New York literary scene, and the metaphor of the web. The final section is personal; it includes an interview, a few of my own poems (in the context of a piece on poetry and dreams), and two short fragments of what might be called memoir.

What holds these disparate pieces together? They overlap, for one thing. Merrill turns up, for example, in "The Ark of What has Been" as well as in the pieces devoted to his work. Greek literature leaves tracks everywhere; not only do I mention Cavafy when discussing Merrill, and vice versa, but in writing about Mona Van Duyn I find myself reminded of Aristophanes. This overlapping seems to indicate that, despite the chronological span between Homer and Mona Van Duyn, my preoccupations cluster in a consistent way. Or maybe it's not so much a matter of preoccupations as of temperament. I suspect that my approach is both personal and bookish—personal when I'm writing about books and bookish when I'm writing about people, address books, web pages, or wells.

Over the years I've written many reviews of books of contemporary poetry. These haven't cost me much of a pang to omit from this slim volume. What seemed important to include were pieces written out of feeling—love for James Merrill or Alan Ansen (both the men and their work); admiration for the poetry of Homer, Cavafy, or Karyotakis. One of the pieces included here, on the other hand, was written in a spirit of indignation: "The Ark of What Has Been" is a kind of counterattack. "Two Letters from New York" and "Tangled Web Sites" take bemused looks at literary or cultural landscapes. Finally, the interview and the other pieces in the last section tend to look inward rather than outward.

I am very grateful to the University of Michigan Press's Poets on Poetry series for making this collection possible, as well as to the editors of the journals in which these pieces originally appeared for having given them their first homes in print.

Contents

Part IV Close to Home

Part I

Five Greek Poets

Horse-Sensible Criticism
Seth Schein on the Iliad

Something about Seth Schein's *The Mortal Hero* seems to in-
cline even the book's admirers to damn it with faint praise;
thus on the back of the jacket we read that the book is
"unhobbyhorsical," "judicious," interesting," "lucid," "read-
able." All these terms are true enough, but—splendidly poly-
syllabic as *unhobbyhorsical* is—they hardly do justice to a book
that's a small masterpiece of judgment, tact, clarity, economy,
and style. *Small* masterpiece—am I belittling too?

The Mortal Hero has a decorum, a modesty even, rarely met
with in the world of academic publishing—a world in which
many books could aptly be described in terms the opposite of
the ones we've just seen (*hobbyhorsical, obfuscatory, unreadable,
unreliable, useless*). Many, if not most, university press books—
those about literature at any rate—fill what has been called a
much-needed gap. If the ideas don't provoke puzzlement or
yawns, then the prose is sure to. (May I indulge in two brief
excerpts, from recent books out from, respectively, Cornell
and Harvard? (1) "Doubts . . . about the efficacy of narrative
as a vehicle for self-reflexive representation and about the
unity and cohesiveness of the psychological subject surface in
a number of modern self-reflexive texts." (2) "It is the inability
not to register the convergence of contradictory motives, com-
bined with the sense of the final mysteriousness of desire,
that . . ." But by then I'd lost interest.)

Schein's book offers a discrete subject, firmly delineated in

---

From *Threepenny Review*, no. 22 (summer 1985).

his preface, and—mirabile dictu—held to. It also and inseparably offers a style. Schein conducts his perspicacious and sensitive analysis of the *Iliad* in a manner that could serve as a model of control, precision, and clarity. Luminously simple, this style never draws attention to itself: Schein doesn't raise his voice in hyperbole, doesn't propound his thesis shrilly, doesn't belabor fellow Homerists with the cudgels of irony. But the way *The Mortal Hero* is written is a crucial ingredient; it is part of what makes the book so pleasant, as well as enlightening, to read. Possibly a sense of Schein's stylistic moderation underlies such praise as *unhobbyhorsical;* it is through the "low tones that decide" (Emerson's phrase in "Uriel") that we come to trust the author's sense.

And not only sense, sensibility. *The Mortal Hero* deals with how and why the *Iliad* is a great work of art; and Schein conveys the poignancy and elaborateness of the poem with a controlled complexity of his own. Without, as I've said, using any of his insights as a stick with which to beat other studies of the *Iliad,* Schein repeatedly shows us why the richest and most rewarding view of the persons and events in the poem is also the complex and tragic view. He is never reductive, simplistic, or faddish. Above all, Schein is balanced in his reading and interpretation, as we realize if we compare other more extreme or partisan readings of the poem. *The Mortal Hero* makes use, for example, of Rachel Bespaloff's memorable insights about some of the epic's personages. But turn to Bespaloff's book, and it seems exaggerated, breathy, and dated; Schein has extracted what is most useful and put it in an illuminating context. Even more to the point, Schein shows that Simone Weil's passionately indignant reading of the poem, true as it is, is incomplete; and he goes on to accomplish the difficult task of making the *Iliad* seem *more* tragic, more dreadful than what Weil perceives in the poem, precisely because the *Iliad* is a work in which (as *The Mortal Hero* never tires of showing us) the elements are inextricably mixed. Tradition and innovation; love of war and horror of war; the splendor and the wretchedness of the human condition—somehow the *Iliad,* instead of bouncing back and forth or stretching taut between these dialectical oppositions, is enriched by being inscrutably poised between them.

The Mortal Hero sent me back to the poem with new attention and awe; it also taught me to teach it better. One of the book's strengths is its availability to readers at every level of expertise, from the college freshman to the classical scholar. All Schein's salient points can be grasped with a greater or lesser degree of literary and philological sophistication. The organization of the book is such that any individual chapter is a self-contained and useful unit. Useful, too, is the way Schein keeps returning the reader to the text of the poem. The passages he examines, whether as famous as the killing of Lykaon in book 21 or as relatively obscure as the death of Simoesios in book 4, are always both noteworthy in themselves and paradigmatic in some way of the entire poem.

So richly structured and endlessly suggestive a work of art, moving yet subtle, tragic yet ambiguous, is (Schein makes the point early on, and it remains crucial) not a primitive Ur-epic of the West. Whatever its place on the syllabus may make us think, the *Iliad* is the end product, not the beginning, of a tradition. It's indicative of Schein's low-key manner that he maintains a scrupulous evenness of tone when pointing out what he clearly feels should be blatantly obvious:

> the fact that the *Iliad* is the product of oral, formulaic composition does not mean that it is therefore unoriginal or inartistic . . .
> a poet in command of his medium could manipulate these building blocks to say whatever he wished: a poor, unimaginative poet would produce poor, unimaginative songs, as would such a poet writing, for example, in English iambic pentameters; a great, imaginative poet like Homer would produce correspondingly great, imaginative poetry, as would Shakespeare.

To make this seemingly obvious point isn't supererogatory, Schein continues,

> because one result of the discovery that the Homeric poems are composed in a traditional style, which enabled illiterate singers to create and perform heroic poetry, has been the conviction

among some Homeric scholars that it is impossible to speak of the artistry or originality of any particular poet, including Homer, who composed in this style, and that it is equally impossible to speak of the meaning of the *Iliad* as a whole or even of many of the individual words.

Showing how what he regards as a fundamental misconception arose, Schein discusses Parry and Lord's work on formulaic verse with his usual economy and clarity. Beyond the interest of the subject is the larger application of the question of whether we can ever assume that a literary work has meaning. It isn't only Homeric scholars who claim that a poet's responsibility for a text is (as Schein paraphrases some Homerists) "incidental" and "cannot be specified." Precisely because Homer can never be more than a name, some would argue, he ("he") is the very model of the modern author, or indeed any author, whose presence we create out of our own anxiety and then proceed to elevate into a myth or a monument. Look again, these critics would say; literature has no meaning but what we supply, no pattern but what we trace ourselves.

The Mortal Hero shows eloquently that what's impossible when we read the *Iliad* is to *deny* meaning, to deny creative purpose and design. Schein makes the vivid, subtle pattern of the poem appear, now brilliantly and now mutedly, but always woven into the fabric of the epic and not to be dismissed as traditional or ignored as incidental. Homer's identity and intention are not the point, but the radiance of the poem's meaning is; and to cancel out such radiance of meaning in the interest of a particular theory is, this book shows us, a form of blindness. Not that Schein puts it so dramatically. "This book," he writes in the preface, "is a literary study of the *Iliad* . . . throughout I have emphasized what is thematically, ethically, and artistically distinctive in the *Iliad* in contrast to the conventions of the poetic tradition of which it is an end product." In doing so, he has taught us a great deal, both about the poem for which his love becomes contagious and about how to read a masterpiece of literature. Unhobbyhorsical, yes; also masterful; and finally, in its understated way, an extremely moving book.

The Quintessential Cavafy

At the funeral of Jacqueline Kennedy Onassis in May 1994, Mrs. Onassis's companion, Maurice Tempelsman, read C. P. Cavafy's poem "Ithaka." The poem was subsequently printed in its entirety in the *New York Times,* whereupon so many intrigued readers apparently rushed to their bookstores that Princeton University Press reprinted its *Collected Poems of C. P. Cavafy,* translated by Edmund Keeley and Philip Sherrard, which had first appeared in 1975.

At 262 pages, the *Collected Cavafy* was hardly a hefty tome. But now Ecco Press has given us, in *The Essential Cavafy,* selected and introduced by Keeley and using the same Keeley-Sherrard translations, what might be called the quintessential work (about forty small pages of poetry) of a poet whose oeuvre is already highly distilled. The notion of an essential Cavafy is in some ways an odd one. Unlike some other poets in Ecco's *Essential* series (Robinson and Browning, Hardy and Whitman come to mind), Cavafy was not a prolific writer. In addition, he was a severe judge of his own work, his own most draconian editor. In his useful introduction to this little book Keeley describes Cavafy's

> idiosyncratic mode of promulgating his work. He never offered a volume of poems for sale during his lifetime. And a number of good poems of his maturity actually remained unpublished in any form, kept among his papers for possible revision at some later date. . . . Those poems that Cavafy allowed to be printed during his lifetime were distributed to a restricted audience. He would pass them out as they seemed ready to his

---

From *New England Review* (winter 1996).

trusted friends first in sample pamphlets, then as broadsheets and offprints, these usually gathered into folders that could be supplemented regularly, some of the older poems revised by hand now and then, a few suppressed. And when the clips in the folders could no longer bear the burden of additional poems, the poet would withdraw some and have them sewn into booklets. He died at seventy without having published a collected edition of his work, presumably because he did not consider it ready yet for that kind of permanent definition. He is reported to have said during his last days that he still had at least twenty-five poems to write, and his archive held a number that he apparently considered still in draft form.

None of this means, of course, that an *Essential Cavafy* is unwelcome. Keeley's carefully chosen and skillfully translated examples can only whet the appetites of those new to this unique poet. But one result of Cavafy's scrupulous standards for his own work, standards he held to over a lifetime, is that all of his poems could be said to be essential.

What was the nature of the life out of which these poems grew? Born in 1863 into a large mercantile family in Alexandria, Egypt, Cavafy was seven years old when his father died and the family began what James Merrill refers to as "years of displacement from one Unreal City to another." Cavafy spent some time in his youth in Constantinople but returned to his native city, where for thirty years he was employed as a clerk in the Ministry of Public Works and where, in 1933, he died. In a splendid 1975 essay (in fact, a review of the *Collected Cavafy*) James Merrill observes that "half Cavafy's life was over before he met, in Athens, any real authors."

The imagination, the preoccupations, and the style of this (unreal?) author are, once Cavafy found his distinctive voice, remarkably of a piece, instantly recognizable, as W. H. Auden noted, even in translation. This homogeneity does not mean that Cavafy has only one subject. His oeuvre, however, appears to offer more variety than, on closer inspection, it turns out to contain—a fact that, far from making Cavafy's world feel claustrophobic, mysteriously enriches it instead. The *Essential Cavafy* (Keeley has arranged his thirty-nine chosen poems chronologically) contains, near the beginning, a few poems that both emerge from and cast a searching light upon scenes or themes from the Homeric epics. "The Horses of Achilles" and "The Trojans" belong to this group, and so, in a way, does the famous "Ithaka." But the latter poem's use of the second person and its avoidance of Odysseus' name fling the gates of reference wide open: these are traveling instructions for anyone who can use them. One such person may have been Mrs. Onassis. Wayne Koestenbaum, in his recent *Jackie under My Skin: Interpreting an Icon*, neatly anatomizes the use Maurice Tempelsman, or some of Tempelsman's listeners, made of the poem:

> reading the C. P. Cavafy poem "Ithaka," he artfully resummoned her years in Greece with Ari. It was wonderfully contrary to the spirit of the mawkish and idealizing media coverage that Jackie's Jewish companion should have chosen a poem celebrating the louche and sybaritic virtues for which Jackie O., in the tabloids, had long been recognized. Of particular interest were the lines: "may you stop at Phoenician trading stations / to buy fine things, / mother of pearl and coral, amber and ebony, / sensual perfume of every kind"—a passage confirming and blessing those acquisitive aspects of Jackie's reputation that the media momentarily neglected.

Distinctively Cafavian as "Ithaka's" reference to "sensual perfume of every kind" is, the slight shrug at the end of the poem, at once ironic and reassuring, is equally characteristic:

> And if you find her poor, Ithaka won't have fooled you.
> Wise as you will have become, so full of experience,
> you will have understood by then what these Ithakas mean.

This shrug, or, to put it in more poetic terms, this piercingly understated note, occurs again far more chillingly at the close of what may be Cavafy's best-known poem, "Waiting for the Barbarians." In this poem the townspeople have gathered apprehensively in the forum, but it finally transpires that the barbarians they so anxiously await will not come—that indeed perhaps "there are no barbarians any longer." The poem ends by asking:

And now, what's going to happen to us without barbarians?
They were, these people, a kind of solution.

As "Waiting for the Barbarians" suggests, Cavafy does not restrict his sources to myth. He also draws heavily, almost greedily, on history. Merrill tells us that Cavafy praised his favorite historians—Herodotus, Plutarch, Gibbon, and various Byzantine chroniclers—for "writing a kind of history that had never been written before. They wrote history dramatically." Developing hints and further dramatizing scenes from such writers, Cavafy is especially adept at locating the point where myth and history meet. Or is it where they part? In "The God Abandons Antony" (the poem's title is a quotation from Plutarch's *Life of Mark Antony*) there is a vivid, almost Shakespearean sense of character and occasion. But the use of the second person and the wistfulness of the poem's cadences ("say goodbye to her, the Alexandria you are losing") peel away the specifics of chronology. Particularities of time and place similarly melt away in "Ionic," the brief poem that follows "The God Abandons Antony" in *The Essential Cavafy:*

> That we've broken their statues,
> that we've driven them out of their temples,
> doesn't mean at all that the gods are dead.
> O land of Ionia, they're still in love with you,
> their souls still keep your memory.
> When an August dawn wakes over you,
> your atmosphere is potent with their life,
> and sometimes a young ethereal figure,
> indistinct, in rapid flight,
> wings across your hills.

Walt Whitman, a poet Cavafy admired, put it this way in "Crossing Brooklyn Ferry: "it avails not, / time nor space avails not." They do not avail in "Ithaka"; they do not avail in "Alexandrian Kings," a poem in which "The Alexandrians turned out in force" to admire the sons of Cleopatra by Caesar and Mark Antony—the winningly theatrical spectacle of a doomed dynasty that is not without resonances of Camelot, the myth (or icon, as Wayne Koestenbaum would call it) preferred by the Kennedy clan.

Mythical echoes and historical references are crucial components of Cavafy's vision, of that ineffable quality variously called his myth (Keeley), his unique perspective on the world (Auden), or, most famously, his standing at a slight angle to the universe (E. M. Forster). Myth and history do not, however, tell the whole story of Cavafy's world. Eros, seldom far below the surface, often lurking around a corner, is needed to complete the story. It is the distinctive triangulation of history, myth, and eros that characterizes some of Cavafy's most resonant work. True, some of the erotic poems, with their deliberate narrowing of focus, seem designed to exclude the public, impersonal dimensions of history and time. But time, it turns out, is not so easily ignored. Cavafy is a master of contrasting scales; we move effortlessly in his work from "A Large Greek Colony" or the crowd scene in "Alexandrian Kings" to a close-up such as we find at the conclusion of "The Bandaged Shoulder."

> When he left, I found, in front of his chair,
> a bloody rag, part of the dressing,
> a rag to be thrown straight into the garbage;
> and I put it to my lips
> and kept it there a long while—
> the blood of love against my lips.

A glance at the titles of the erotic poems included in *The Essential Cavafy* shows that time has made its stealthy way into almost all of them: "Since Nine O'Clock," "The Afternoon Sun," "Days of 1896," "Days of 1908," "Half an Hour." Even—perhaps especially—in the bedroom, it is a certain time of day, a certain year. An encounter has duration (say half an hour); then, relegated to memory, desire takes its place in the mythistorical perspective.

Sometimes Cavafy strikes all three of his crucial notes simultaneously, as in "Myris: Alexandria, A.D. 340," where the historical clash of Hellenism and Christianity is embodied both in the beautiful youth Myris and in the speaker of the poem, who is mourning Myris's death. But even in shorter and apparently less ambitious poems, it is rare to find only a single dimension. Cavafy's unadorned language, his famous eschewing of the figurative—these distinctive traits are inseparable from qualities harder to capture in words but equally essential or quintessential: his profound worldliness, his deep ironies, his sly humor, and most of all, perhaps, his refusal to oversimplify. Even lovelorn, Cavafy retains the sense of the larger world outside the bedroom; even conjuring a crowd, he notes the distinctive impulses and desires that ripple through its individual members.

Fittingly for this deeply private and profoundly public poet, Cavafy was a favorite writer of the deeply private and profoundly public Jacqueline Onassis. Equally fitting, we learned of this affinity only after Mrs. Onassis's death. Another, less secret Cavafy fan has already made an appearance here—the great poet James Merrill, who also died not long ago. And, although Cavafy hardly ever uses metaphor in his poems and Merrill almost always does, nevertheless it is Merrill who gave us, in the poems he wrote in Greece in the 1960s and 1970s, some of the most beautiful homages to this now very popular poet. (Cavafy doesn't lack for admirers these days; but many writers who evoke him—I think of Mark Doty's *My Alexandria,* and there are many others—conspicuously lack his wide-angled, dry worldliness.) The very title of Merrill's "Days of 1964," a love poem set in the American poet's Athenian neighborhood, recalls Cavafy; so too, most strongly, do some lines near the end of the poem: "Where I hid my face, your touch, quick, merciful, / Blindfolded me. A god breathed from my lips." And the poem ends, "But you were everywhere beside me, masked, / As who was not, in laughter, pain, and love."

It is a benignly Cavafian irony that one path into Cavafy's world is death. Jacqueline Onassis's funeral may have opened the door to Cavafy for many people; at least one memorial tribute to Merrill mentioned the poet's affinities to Cavafy. "Death is the mother of beauty," wrote Wallace Stevens, a poet at his own angle to the universe. And in a poem not collected here (Keeley's choices are superb, but what can he do with a poet whose corpus is already so concentrated?), "Melancholy

of Jason Kleander, Poet in Kommagini, A.D. 595," Cavafy
wrote:

> The aging of my body and my beauty
> is a wound from a merciless knife. . . .
>
> Bring your drugs, Art of Poetry—
> they do relieve the pain at least for a while.

Enjoying the Funeral

Konstantine Karyotakis

Readers of modern Greek poetry in English need no longer
limit themselves to Cavafy and Seferis. Fresh translations of
Sikelianos and Ritsos have recently appeared; since the 1979
Nobel Prize much Elytis is available; and now, thanks to the
indefatigable Kimon Friar, we can also enjoy work by Takis
Sinopoulos and Miltos Sahtouris.

Meanwhile, a fascinating figure has gotten lost in the
shuffle. Konstantine Karyotakis (1896–1928) is probably the
Greek poet of this century least likely to be translated into
English. So staunchly does Karyotakis defy translation that
Edmund Keeley and Philip Sherrard were forced to omit him
from their important anthology, *Voices of Modern Greece*. This is
a real loss. Karyotakis has strong claims on lovers of lyric poetry,
including a superlative ear for the rhythms and tones and gra-
dations of Greek in its various guises (among them bureau-
cratese and such imports as *Kodak* and *lorgnette*); a technical and

---

From *Grand Street* (autumn 1983).

At the time I wrote this essay, in 1982–83, I knew of no verse
translation of Konstantine Karyotakis and thus supplied my own
unrhymed, plain-jane renderings. In 1990–91, however, I took cour-
age to translate fifteen poems of Karyotakis into rhymed, stanzaic
versions (these can be found in my 1994 book of translations, *Other
Worlds than This*). Hence, in revising the present essay, I have inserted
my verse translations of "Military March," "Justification," "Mother
and Son," and "Preveza."

The Greek edition is G. P. Savidis, ed., *K. G. Karyotakis: Poiemata
kai Peza* (Athens: Nea Elliniki Vivliothiki, 1977).

formal mastery equal to that of any other writer in the language; and a uniquely dapper, flickering gloom.

The verbal effects are of course what make translation difficult. A Greek man of letters once commented glumly on Seferis's expert exegeses of Seferis's own work: "The only man in Greece who is a good enough critic to understand the poetry of Seferis is Seferis himself." And perhaps only Karyotakis would be capable of translating the poetry of Karyotakis adequately. About a sixth of Karyotakis's oeuvre consists of brilliant translations of Villon, Gautier, Corbière, Heine, and others. A successful rendering of the Greek poet's work would require the kind of perfection that his translations achieve: accurate sense, yes, but also intact rhyme schemes, an elegantly idiomatic use of the translator's tongue, and an indescribable wash of elegance over the whole.

If poetry is what gets lost in translation, then Cavafy, Seferis, and Elytis are not poets. All these writers in their various ways triumphantly survive translation; but not so their stubborn colleague. Nor is this the only way Karyotakis is out of step. He is also largely indifferent to the rich resources of the Hellenic ambiance and past—history, mythology, even landscape. Cavafy, it is true, does without the natural world. But take from Cavafy's work its long historical perspective; deprive Seferis or Elytis or Sikelianos of the dimensions of either myth or landscape, and the resulting work will be obscenely truncated. Erase history, mythology, or for that matter nine tenths of the natural world from Karyotakis, and what's left is not a sad remnant but rather—in its entirety—the vision of a poet whose imagination (turning Donne's phrase around) makes an everywhere one little room.

Generally, that room is either an office or a bed-sitter—though the language of a poem like "Office," with its echo of Verlaine's "Le Ciel est, par-dessus le toit," certainly hints at a prison:

> The hours have sallowed me, again bent over
> my disagreeable desk.
> (From the open window onto the opposite wall
> sunlight glides, plays.)

> Doubling up my chest, I gasp for breath
> in the dust of my papers.
> (Sweetly life throbs and, thousand-voiced, is heard
> in the freedom of the street.)

Karyotakis's office workers are, like the poet himself, civil servants—in a skewed way, professional writers. They suffer double alienation: the office cuts them off from the sunlit world of throbbing life, and the enforced use of *katharevousa* (officialese) cuts them off from the normal use of language. For a man whose métier is language, the endless copying out of phrases like "I have the honor, esteemed sir, to be . . . " surely becomes as stifling as the stale air of the office.

A poet whose flowers are more likely to bloom in vases or buttonholes than in gardens has clear affinities with the restrictions and ingenuities imposed by form. Karyotakis is not merely at home in formal verse; he luxuriates there, among sonnets, ballads, rhymed fifteen-syllable couplets, unrhymed hendecasyllabics, four-line stanzas of various kinds, and other forms of his own invention (there are also prose poems). His rhymes, feminine because of the polysyllabic nature of Greek, are a constant pleasure—and about as easily rendered as Byron's "intellectual / hen peck'd you all." Sometimes the rhymes alone create ironic contrasts that operate like minipoems. "Military March, Mournful and Vertical" is (as we shall see) a poem about deflated aspirations, coming to terms with limits. The rhymes keep up a sly commentary on the notion of sublimity, or simply height (Longinus' *Peri Hypsous* means literally "On the High Style"). *Hypsous*—loftiness—is made to rhyme in this poem with *gypsous* (plaster); *horis uphos* (without style) rhymes with *katakoryphos* (vertically)—a little chime of incongruity. In "All Together," a poem about poets and poetry, the *abba* rhyme scheme is neatly used to frame the two middle rhymes (*kardiá mas / poiematá mas*) (our hearts / our poems) with *syllavés/poités* (syllables/poets)—so that the actual syllables, tools of the trade, and the writers themselves are made to surround the poems that are the heart of the matter. Elsewhere in the same poem the wonderfully resonant word for rhyme (*omoiokatalexía*) rhymes with *philodoxia*—ambition (the ambition, of course, to write great poems). In a transformation (rather than a translation) of François Villon's "Ballad of Dead Ladies" into a lay for dead poets, Karyotakis produces a series of verbs to rhyme with *pou'ne* (where are they): *methoune* (they get drunk), *stichourgoune* (they write verses), *ksehnoune* (they forget), and *poune* (they say), "they" being of course the vanished poets.

"Military March," referred to earlier, is a meditation on the restrictions and consolations of form.

> Meander patterns on the ceiling's white
> into their plaster dance are drawing me.
> The happiness I feel must be
> a matter of height.
>
> Symbols of transcendency abound:
> a wheel of mystic power,
> a white acanthus flower,
> and the sculpted horn they both surround.
>
> Humble art without the least pretense,
> I learn your lesson late,
> dream molded in relief which I can sense
> only in terms of height.
>
> Too many boundaries are choking me.
> In every clime and latitude,
> struggles for one's daily bread,
> love affairs, ennui.
>
> But let me now put on
> that handsome plaster crown.
> Thus bordered by the ceiling I shall be
> a splendid sight to see.

The setting is one of those closed rooms that provide a measure of refuge from the tedium of the office. Tellos Agras has observed that these bleak interiors are the poet's "only group of friends, silent and gloomy: inanimate objects . . . furniture, the interiors of houses. [Karyotakis] loves undisturbedly things which are themselves undisturbed, immoveable, sealed with chilly dust as if immobilized by the past." Windows are a recurring image: through them the outside world is at once framed, removed, and accessible. Ideal suicides, in a poem of that title, "stand at the window, see / trees, children, nature, / hear marble workers hammering away."

"Military March," then, is scaled to this solitary room. But the poem explores the limits of form as well as of a space—stanza, after all, means both a room and a unit of poetry. Smallness, the poet finds, is "delightful"—but the conclusion is not reached without struggle, sacrifice, and irony. A constant theme in Karyotakis is the wrestling of slightness with intensity.

This poem is one of several that recall Kafka's world of offices and solitaries. Karyotakis's literary affinities would make a curious study. They stretch from Gogol and Chekhov to Kafka, Rimbaud, Poe, and the Melville of "Bartleby." Whether the Greek poet had actually read any of these writers except presumably Rimbaud and Poe, I have no idea.

Karyotakis's most celebrated trait is his profound, nearly unremitting gloom—a gloom always in danger of toppling over into the ludicrous, as when the poet draws a skull and crossbones as the frontispiece of his last book, *Elegies and Satires*. Or does the satirical side of the poetry simply poke fun at the elegiac? Certainly, Karyotakis's choice of an epigraph for this volume is comically incongruous. The quote is from that cheery poet Lucretius: "Et metus ille foras praeceps Acheruntis agendus/funditus humanam qui vitam turbat ab imo." (It must be cast out head first, that fear of death which so profoundly disturbs human life.) Fear of death is central for Lucretius, but Karyotakis's problem is a little different. Life, not death, "profoundly disturbs" our poet, for whom cessation is usually a consummation devoutly to be wished. Life means loneliness, ennui, ill health—the office, the bed-sitter, the dying garden. Death not only provides a tranquil haven from all this; it also confers importance. Encoffined and borne aloft, the physically puny poet will (at long last) no longer be able to be dismissed as a lightweight:

> When we slowly hit the road
> they'll find that I'm a heavy load
> (for the first time) on four men's backs.

Taking over my life's strain
finally, shovelfuls will rain
beautifully down upon me: thorns, clods, rocks.
                                                ("Justification")

Karyotakis was literally a lightweight. His misery and isola-
tion, his oscillations between self-pity and bitter contempt,
cannot be separated from his frail, tubercular, prematurely
withered body. Photographs show a man whose short legs,
hollow chest, and high shoulders are incongruously topped by
a massive, distinguished-looking head that seems to belong
somewhere else—a fact acknowledged by the expression of
disdainful surprise. One poem refers directly to what must
have been a constant burden, when the twenty-four-year-old
poet tells his younger brother:

You have grown up. But I remain the same.
The years have passed, but they have left me still
a weird, withered little old boy/man. (*paraxeno paidaki
    yerasmeno*)

Nor was it only Karyotakis's stature that remained undevel-
oped. There is something adolescent about his self-pity, his
recurrent wish to wreak vengeance on an uncaring world. An
unusually dramatic poem locates the source of the trouble in a
family relation:

—My love, you were a child; my child, you are a man now.
Go on, my darling, do not let the tempest overtake you.

—Mother, look, night has fallen. How can I go? It's raining.
Mother, sorrow keeps me here, a kind of terror clamps me.

The dialogue goes on for another seven stanzas, but clearly
the mother will never be able to pry her son loose from his
enclosure and get him out into the world. One pities, and
shuns, them both.

If Karyotakis did not even begin in gladness, no one was

more aware of it than the poet himself. A little poem called "Criticism" labels the whole oeuvre a cry of pain:

> This is no longer a song. It is not even the sound
> of a human voice. It is like
> the last howl, deep in the night,
> of someone who has died.

But this is about as accurate as Roethke's claim that "Rage warps my clearest cry / To witless agony." True, Karyotakis's poems do come to have the remorseless logic of a last gesture; the impulse that elicits them will presently silence them. But the language is a far cry from being raw or unformed. Karyotakis wrote the way he dressed, with a formal flair that persisted, if only through sheer habit, to the very end.

That end happened to come in Preveza, a small provincial town where Karyotakis was assigned a bureaucratic post apparently as the result of some feud with a superior in the Civil Service. The enemy responsible for the transfer must have found his revenge embarrassingly speedy and complete. Karyotakis arrived in Preveza on June 18, 1928, and on July 21 he shot himself. A photograph of the dead man taken by local authorities shows a natty figure reclining under a tree, apparently asleep. The poet is clad in a three-piece suit. His straw hat has been decorously placed on his waistcoated chest. He wears, in addition, a look of profound distaste.

"Preveza," if not the final poem in the canon, is a celebrated shudder of revulsion whose ending neatly matches and foreshadows the end of the life:

> If at least one person from this place
> from horror, boredom, and disgust would drop,
> silent and solemn, each with a long face,
> at the funeral we'd all live it up.

But it is hardly fair to blame the revulsion or the suicide on dull little Preveza. Karyotakis had been drowsy for death (*yia thanato nistazo*) from the beginning. He had also been witty and original from the beginning—and witty and original he remained. "Preveza" is very funny in its own poker-faced way. Humdrum details (official place-names; such routine errands of a newcomer in town as opening a bank account) are fitted with perfect simplicity into a deadpan litany that—I can testify—unliterary Greeks still recite with glee.

> Ah, Preveza, fortress and garrison!
> On Sunday we'll go listen to the band.
> I got a savings booklet from the bank.
> First deposit: thirty drachmas down.
>
> Strolling slowly up and down the quay,
> "Do I exist?" you say. "You're not alive!"
> Here comes the steamer, and her flag flies high.
> His Excellency the Governor may arrive.

No other Greek poet before had thought of including ho-hum matters like the amount of a deposit in a poem at all, let alone a poem of such underlying Hamlet-like despair. Moreover, the words for bank and drachmas are in *katharevousa;* it somehow adds to the fun that only a white-collar type would ever dream of saying *drachmai* instead of *drachmes, trapézis* instead of *trápezas.* One image in another stanza gives us a glimpse of a civil servant indignantly weighing his dinner at Preveza Police Headquarters because he suspects his government-allotted portion of being too small (*ellipi,* katharevousa for insufficient). We seem closer to the world of Gogol or Chekhov than to a suicidal lyric poem.

Where might Karyotakis's work have gone, if only he had held out against the drowsiness of death? Greek critics have speculated on various possibilities: satire, criticism, translation—genres tending toward prose. But the laconic idiom of Karyotakis's slender poetic oeuvre already accommodates at least the germs of all these literary forms, on a small but flawless scale. Perhaps one day a translator will let more readers into those musty rooms, allow a wider audience to catch the ironic glint behind the gloom. In any case it is good to know that this constricted, idiosyncratic, and splendid poet is alive and well in paperback—in Greek.

Wildly Obstinate, Always Wounded

The mature poetry of George Seferis (1900–1971) does not depend for its effect on beautiful sounds, complex wordplay, or unreproduceable rhymes. Seferis's crucial quality is that unfashionable thing known as voice, and the good news for English-speaking readers is that the voice comes through pretty much unscathed in Keeley and Sherrard's excellent translations. This weighty, deliberate voice—it is part of the not-so-good news about Seferis—becomes stalled from time to time by its own ponderousness, entrapped by its habitual gravity; but slowness and monotony are the concomitants of the power of this poetry. More troubling is a certain tiredness about the whole enterprise. Seferis's oeuvre sometimes seems to lose its quiddity and blend into what might be called International Glum Modernism. Those crumbling statues and devastated landscapes in Seferis—we've seen something like them in the empty piazzas and headless figurines of de Chirico. That endless voyage that is Seferis's recurring emblem—it recalls not only Homer and Vergil and Apollonius but Pound. Above all, that weary, aging voice sounds a great deal like much of *Four Quartets.*

Just what makes Seferis special, then—not only in the sense that he won the Nobel Prize in 1968 and is still revered in Greece but in the sense that he speaks to us now? Language alone can't be the answer, given this poet's almost embarrassing accessibility to translation. Seferis's Greek is colloquial but

From *Pequod* 26/27 (1989).

Translations cited are from *George Seferis: Collected Poems,* translated, edited, and introduced by Edmund Keeley and Philip Sherrard, expanded edition (Princeton: Princeton University Press, 1981).

not informal; laconic without sacrificing sonority; grave; austere. One falls back on the notion of voice: Seferis flirts with facelessness and wins by losing. Through his poetic voice he achieves a limited, authentic sublimity.

As it happens, I did once hear Seferis read (at Harvard in 1968), and I retain a very clear memory of a remark he made in English: "Had I not been a poet, I would wish to have been a geographer." It's a thought I'll return to later. The speaking voice was deep, slow, rich, almost but not quite too plummy for an edge of irony to shimmer through.

The voice is the key to the strengths and weaknesses of an oeuvre that has probably been both overpraised and undervalued. Seferis's slow pace creates—and needs—lots of room for spaces, silences, lacunae; the discontinuous mode of the long poem comes naturally to him. The twenty-four-part sequence *Mythistorema* (1935)—the word translates as "mythical history" but also means "novel" in modern Greek—is Seferis's best-known and his most sustainedly successful poem, partly because of his affinity for the loose sequential form. It illustrates the rewards of Seferis's poetry and shows some of its limitations.

At its best *Mythistorema* has the kind of inevitability few poets ever manage to capture—as if the words had always been there. There seems to be no contrivance, coyness, artifice: nothing is here that isn't needed, and it all seems true.

> Three rocks, a few burnt pines, a solitary chapel
> and farther above
> the same landscape repeated starts again:
> three rocks in the shape of a gate-way, rusted,
> a few burnt pines, black and yellow,
> and a square hut buried in whitewash;
> and still farther above, many times over,
> the same landscape recurs level after level
> to the horizon, to the twilit sky.
>
> Here we moored the ship to splice the broken oars,
> to drink water and sleep.
> The sea that embittered us is deep and unexplored
> and unfolds a boundless calm.

Here among the pebbles we found a coin
and threw dice for it.
The youngest won it and disappeared.

We set out again with our broken oars.

(Mythistorema 12)

But these moments remain isolated; the separate sections
do not build on one another. If we try to read *Mythistorema* as a
narrative, we'll be almost as baffled as if we were trying to
make a logical outline of *Notes Toward a Supreme Fiction*.
Seferis's story of a voyage is as much of a disguise as Stevens's
lecture on aesthetics; both poems must be turned like jewels so
we can admire facets, but they don't deploy themselves in
time, according to the logic of narrative or argument. *Mythist-
orema* ends nowhere in particular; the very verb tenses are
confusing, and Seferis's pronouns are almost as slippery as
Ashbery's. The first six sections of the sequence, for example,
move from the first person plural (the person and number
finally most congenial to the deep, blurry, collective voice of
this poetry) to second person singular, first person singular,
third person plural, back to second person singular.

When Seferis—rather rarely—risks saying "I," his writing
can be at its strongest. Consider the third section of *Mythistor-
ema*, which could surely stand alone.

Remember the baths where you were murdered

I woke with this marble head in my hands;
it exhausts my elbows and I don't know where to put it down.
It was falling into the dream as I was coming out of the dream
so our life became one and it will be very difficult for it
to disunite again.

I look at the eyes: neither open nor closed
I speak to the mouth which keeps trying to speak
I hold the cheeks which have broken through the skin.
I don't have any more strength.

My hands disappear and come toward me
mutilated.

This passage shows how Seferis's preoccupations can lock into his power. The crushing sense of belatedness, loneliness, paralysis, even mutilation—all this is palpably conveyed but at the same time effortlessly metaphorical. It's impossible to read the heavy head as merely a hunk of marble; what is also weighing the speaker down is tradition, guilt, whatever we make of inheritance. The point is that, like the epigraph from Aeschylus' *The Libation Bearers,* the heavy head comes packed with sinister associations. This is true of Seferis's poetry in general, at its most evocative; in "The King of Asine," for example, the search is as much for a word, a memory, a lost language, as it is for some tangible relic. Abstractions assume concrete guise but equally the simplest act radiates symbolic significance. Seferis talks a good deal in his prose of the search for simplicity, but it is simplicity of language, of surface, that he is after; the thought is always many-layered. Language must have the strength of simplicity in order not to buckle under the weight of what has come before. Even if they sustain this burden, our words are marked by it:

> When will you speak again?
> Our words are the children of many people.
> They are sown, are born like infants,
> take root, are nourished with blood.
> As pine trees hold the wind's imprint
> after the wind has gone, is no longer there,
> so words
> retain a man's imprint
> after the man is gone, is no longer there.
> ("On Stage," pt. 6, from *Three Secret Poems*)

In two long poems written before he hit his stride with *Mythistorema,* Seferis is preoccupied with the ineffable to the point where words and meaning part company. Not coincidentally, *Erotikos Logos* (1930) and *The Cistern* (1932) are far more resistant to translation than *Mythistorema* or *Three Secret Poems* (1971). As hard to paraphrase as they are to translate, the two poems of the early 1930s might be said to be about the sinuous sonorities of language. If we can discern *La Jeune Parque* through the symbolist hazes, we can also hear, and much more insistently, in *Erotikos Logos* the fifteen-syllable measure of much Greek folk poetry and especially of the Cretan Renaissance epic *Erotokritos*. But Seferis's abstract and elaborate diction, unenlivened by a shred of narrative energy, creates in using this meter as odd an effect of juxtaposition as does Auden's use of Anglo-Saxon alliterative verse in *The Age of Anxiety*. The marriage of old and new remains unconsummated.

One can hardly blame Keeley and Sherrard for not attempting to reproduce the rhyme in *Erotikos Logos* or *The Cistern*, but their loosely metrical version of the former fails to give any idea of the cumulative effect, in the original, of ninety-six lines of da dá da dá da dá da dá da dá da DA da, or: *Tá místiká tis thálassas ksehnioúnte st'ákroyália* (acute accents mark stresses, not Greek orthography). It would have been interesting to see at least an attempt at rendering this obsessive beat, but Keeley and Sherrard refer in a footnote to Seferis's "less characteristic—and less translatable—early phase," which to their credit they include in the volume, relegating their versions of the rhymed poems to the back of the book.

Mythistorema was followed by some striking shorter lyrics in *Logbooks* 2 and 3, but Seferis's most ambitious sequences after *Mythistorema* are both mixed successes. *Thrush* (1950), a sort of long shudder of relief after the horrors of the war, was undoubtedly cathartic for the poet, but it tries to do too much. The sections where Seferis attempts semihumorous vignettes, bits of real life, human drama, are failures; the transcendent finale of the poem, if not wholly successful, is daring, for Seferis's primarily dark imagination turns inside out, giving us "light, angelic and black." What is most beautiful in *Thrush*, though, is not the rather equivocal vision of paradise with which the poem ends but an earlier passage that might easily be inserted into *Mythistorema*. The poet has been pondering the wreckage of the sunken craft "Thrush," but what kindles his imagination is envisioned out of time:

> And the boys who dived from the bow-sprits
> go like spindles twisting still,
> naked bodies plunging into black light

with a coin between the teeth, swimming still,
while the sun with golden needles sews
sails and wet wood and colors of the sea;
even now they're going down obliquely,
the white lekythoi,
towards the pebbles on the sea floor.

Three Secret Poems, Seferis's final work, seems to me more
satisfying than *Thrush,* if spottier than *Mythistorema.* The
twenty-eight separate sections range from the forced melo-
drama of parts of "On Stage" to a poetic terrain where Seferis is
much more at home. Juxtapose two passages like the following
and the effect is jaggedly uneven:

Your eyes were two tragic shells,
two small purple stones
covered your nipples—stages properties, perhaps.
The three bellowed,
you stood rooted to the soil.
Their gesticulations rent the air.

("On Stage," pt. 3)

The sea: how did the sea get like this?
I lingered for years in the mountains;
the fireflies blinded me.
Now, on this beach, I'm waiting for someone to land,
or a piece of flotsam, a raft.

("On Stage," pt. 4)

As soon as the poet abandons his factitious interest in the
unconvincingly lewd details of half-imagined bodies, the voice
is free to become itself, with no hemming, hawing, or per-
hapsing. The uniquely hesitant yet authoritative sound of
Seferis comes through in the passage about the fireflies—a
passage adduced by Peter Levi when he comments accurately
that "the economy and intense power of Seferis's style as it has
developed have limited his range." Seferis's limited range has
the depth of a narrow channel through which the same stream
has repeatedly flowed. His development as a poet consists not

27

in technical experimentation or increasing a repertory of styles but—to change the metaphor in midstream—in repeated, dogged buttings at the bedrock of what he knew.

Seferis called himself, late in life, a *pismatáris*—stubborn old fellow who had only one or two things to say and kept saying them over and over. It isn't as simple as stubbornness, of course. In his journals Seferis bemoans not only the exhaustion caused by his busy professional life as a diplomat but also the way that life pollutes his subconscious. *Thrush*, composed on the island of Poros during the poet's first vacation since the war, was a cathartic poem; the journals note the gradual cleansing during this period of Seferis's dreams. Part of what needed scouring must have been the miasma of *katharevousa*, the officialese of Seferis's daily diplomatic dealings (not to mention French, Seferis's second language, which also crept into his dreams).

To purify the dialect of the tribe was for this poet an arduous, unending personal project. The clear, spare texts of his poems in English inevitably fail to convey the strenuous sense of struggle that evidently accompanied all Seferis's creative activity. His mind, his language, his sense of what that language could say: all can be compared to a palimpsest at which he continually scraped away, seeking lost origins, a forgotten freshness and simplicity. This search explains why Seferis once referred to himself as an autodidact. The term sounds disingenuous from this well-educated man, but what Seferis meant was that his groping progress toward a Greek tradition he could connect with was a lonely, unguided one. Community and isolation, authority and hesitancy, simplicity and exhaustion—his art embraces these apparent opposites.

It hardly needs saying that Seferis's limits are also his strengths. What he does well he has somehow made securely his own; would-be imitators, at least in Greek, always sound like flat parodies. There is one story and one story only, wrote Robert Graves, and this is certainly true of Seferis, though *story* doesn't quite convey his static quality: a moralized landscape or a quest for depths of hidden treasure capture his obsessions better. If it is real Seferis, we might require (*Notes Toward a Supreme Fiction* creeping in again) three essential markings of a poem: it must be tragic; it must be metaphorical; it must be geographical.

For Seferis was telling the truth at Harvard—had he not been a poet (and diplomat), he might indeed have been a geographer. Cavafy, it is well known, said he (Cavafy) might easily have been a historian instead of a poet; and the historian in Cavafy does more than show through the poet, he shapes that poet. For Seferis geography and topography are finally more important than people, though necessarily incomplete without them. Consider some of what Eliot might have called the objective correlatives in Seferis's work. Archaeological excavation; sailing; statues, often faceless; Makriyannis's notion of style as a painstaking putting together of hand-hewn stones; Cyprus, Asine, Poros, or Syngrou Avenue as representative places. Repeatedly, living people are secondary to situation, to site. Similarly, Seferis's prose essays on Delphi and Cappadocia chiefly concern place.

Seferis's resemblances to Eliot are intermittent but striking. In "East Coker" is a passage that not only applies to Seferis's career but might well have been written by him.

> Home is where one starts from. As we grow older
> The world becomes stranger, the pattern more complicated
> Of dead and living. Not the intense moment
> Isolated, with no before and after,
> But a lifetime burning in every moment
> And not the lifetime of one man only
> But of old stones that cannot be deciphered.

If we look for the intense moment isolated in Seferis's poems, we shall be disappointed. But for a kind of prophetic truthfulness, he is irreplaceable. As Peter Levi points out, the sacrifice of lightness, suppleness, and variety was apparently necessary in order for Seferis, at the end of his life, to be able to pack a poem like "The Cats of Saint Nicholas" with its freight of tragic conviction. Typically about history and a place rather than people, this poem is unusual in also being a kind of animal fable. In any case Seferis is up to his old tricks of moral geography. Here is the greater part of the poem.

It was during the great drought,
forty years without rain,
the whole island devastated,
people died and snakes were born.
This cape had millions of snakes
thick as a man's legs
and full of poison.
In those days the monastery of St. Nicholas
was held by the monks of St. Basil,
and they couldn't work their fields,
couldn't put their flocks to pasture.
In the end they were saved by the cats they raised.
Every day at dawn a bell would strike
and an army of cats would move into battle.
They'd fight the day long,
until the bell sounded for the evening feed.
Supper done, the bell would sound again
and out they'd go to battle through the night.
They say it was a marvelous sight to see them,
some lame, some twisted, others missing
a nose, an ear, their hides in shreds.
So to the sound of four bells a day
months went by, years, season after season.
Wildly obstinate, always wounded,
they annihilated the snakes; but in the end they disappeared;
they just couldn't take in that much poison.
Like a sunken ship
they left no trace on the surface:
not a meow, not a bell even.
Steady as you go!
Poor devils, what could they do,
fighting like that day and night, drinking
the poisonous blood of those snakes?
Generations of poison, centuries of poison.
"Steady as you go," indifferently echoed the helmsman.

The poem ends with a date—Wednesday, February 5, 1969—
two years into the 1967–74 junta. Seferis was slow to speak
out, some said at the time; he said nothing in prose until 1971.
But there is this poem. *Chronia pharmáki, yenies pharmáki.* It is
more than an ephemeral political statement; the deep, heavy
voice is that of a prophet telling a timeless truth.

Ritsos's Fourth Dimension

Any cartoon, painting, play, or poem featuring mythological personages can be said to bring them back to life. The striking thing about the seventeen hefty monologues, averaging more than a dozen pages in length, that comprise the late Greek poet Yannis Ritsos's collection *The Fourth Dimension* is not that they reanimate Ajax or Helen, Orestes or Clytemnestra; it's that these figures still seem at least half-dead.

Is Ritsos's fourth dimension death? These long, slow poems deliberately amalgamate the past and the present, the living and the dead. The resulting macédoine is Ritsos's recurrent subject.

> Along with our own food they prepared
> the food for the dead. At the hour when we ate
> they took from the table pitchers with honey and oil
> and carried them to unknown graves. We made no distinction
> between wine jars and funeral vases. We did not know
> what was ours and what belonged to the dead.
>
> ("Philoctetes")

We might expect the cumulative effect to be shock, blasphemy, revelation. Yet it's none of these—it's exhaustion.

Taken singly, virtually any one of Ritsos's leisurely monologues is a reminiscence of a particular mythical episode decked out with cigarettes, coffee cups, and other mild anachronisms. But although the speakers are looking back in time, it isn't hindsight they offer so much as puzzlement: what did it all mean?

From *Boston Review* (Feb.–Mar. 1994).

Yes, they're just as stupid as we are. Only quieter. Another one
lifts his hand in a formal gesture, as though to deliver a eulogy,
cuts a crystal from the chandelier, and places it in his mouth
very simply, like a glass fruit—you think he's going to chew it,
    reactivate
some kind of human function; but no, he just holds it
      between his teeth
so that the crystal glitters with idle brilliance. A woman
scoops face cream out of its round white jar
with a practiced movement of two fingers, and writes
two big thick capital letters—E and Θ, perhaps—
on the windowpane. The sun warms the pane, the cream melts,
    drips down the wall—
this has no significance whatever—in two short greasy tracks.

("Helen")

There are many quick vignettes of sensuality, many mor-
dant speculations, some Proustian reflections on the passage
of time. But read—as Ritsos intended—end to end, the sheer
weight of verbiage in these monologues is overwhelming.
Peter Green and Beverly Bardsley, the excellent translators,
are right to comment in their introduction that:

> It is no accident that the complete collection has never appeared
> in English, that the temptation to present fragments, to excerpt,
> to dilute its impact has been too strong to resist. The book's . . .
> impact is deliberate. At moments we will feel—as we were meant
> to do—that there are too many dead, that they are too large, that
> they go on too long.

I am less convinced by their next remark, that *The Fourth
Dimension* challenges us to confront our own ambivalence to-
ward the Other and toward the past, to ask how many of those
who pray for the resurrection of the dead would truly welcome
it. Maybe so; but I feel chiefly challenged in the area of poetic
decorums and taste, not in my beliefs. I am unable in fact, to
extract much deep insight from *The Fourth Dimension*. This is
not necessarily a criticism; poetry is rarely the place to go for a
revamping of our beliefs. Figures like Orestes or Iphigenia, as
E. R. Dodds pointed out a generation ago in *The Greeks and the*

Irrational, felt threadbare centuries before Christ. Ritsos bears eloquent witness to the shabbiness of the old myths; we must pry out profundity, if there is any, from beneath his deadpan surfaces.

It is in his relentless cataloguing of the ordinary that Ritsos's originality lies. His accomplishment in *The Fourth Dimension* is to string the painted, chipped beads of the everyday onto long, long loops of thread, where they tangle and dangle—striking, yes, but impractical, hard to disengage, and, finally, a bit absurd.

To change the trope from ornament to what lies beneath: despite Ritsos's unerring eye for every kind of detail, his lines have a flabby feeling, languorous and passive as the lives they recount. At times this flaccidity comes across as a lack of affect, at others as eroticism or faint cruelty.

> Let's go further down; I can't bear to hear her, her cries
> batter my nerves and my dreams, just as those oars
> battered the floating slaughtered corpses
> momentarily lit up by the ships' flares, the shooting stars of
>   August,
> and they were all agleam, young and erotic, unbelievably
>   immortal,
> in a watery death that cooled their backs, their ankles, their
>   legs.
>
> ("Orestes")

The constant loneliness, boredom, and nostalgia in which all Ritsos's speakers are steeped may not admit of sentimentality, but it positively fosters garrulity. The fact that there has been no news for two or three millennia prevents no one from nattering on at length. Language, even more than such novelties as ice cream cones or prams, might be thought to be a stimulant to the poor dead; but the truth in these poems is closer to the opposite. Death is at least as contagious as life; a strange lethargy flows back and forth between the two until we can no longer distinguish the one group from the other. Both, after all, inhabit a world in which whatever is going to happen has already happened.

Ritsos's figures recall characters from Homer and the trage-
dians, especially Euripides, rather faintly. Some of Tennessee
Williams's heroines or a ghostly presence like Miss Havisham
are closer kin. But what finally struck me with a pang was that
Ritsos's real subject is not mythology but the pathos and po-
etry of lives that have gone on too long. Grislier than death,
his true fourth dimension is old age.

Part II

Homage to James Merrill

"We Both Knew This Place"

Reflections on the Art of James Merrill

In April 1995, teaching some poems of Elizabeth Bishop in my American Poetry course at Rutgers, I went back to the chapter on Bishop in David Kalstone's *Five Temperaments.* The charm and perspicacity of Kalstone's writing quickly drew me into rereading the rest of the book as well, particularly the chapter on James Merrill. Merrill's death only two months earlier resonated so deeply that the spring semester came to feel to me like an extended course in Merrill's oeuvre, though I was never sure whether it was a course I was taking or one I was giving.

Merrill and Kalstone were close friends for many years. Kalstone wrote about Merrill in *Five Temperaments* and elsewhere; I still remember my pleasure in reading his spirited response to an inadequate review of *Divine Comedies* in 1976. Merrill, for his part, wrote the afterword to *Becoming a Poet,* Kalstone's last book. Sadly, since his illness with AIDS and death in June 1986 prevented Kalstone from finishing it, *Becoming a Poet,* a study of poetic friendships and influences, is both posthumous and incomplete.

Merrill's brief afterword to *Becoming a Poet* was, in light of Kalstone's death, poignant at the time it was written. Now that Merrill too is gone, it is doubly so. On the friendship between Robert Lowell and Elizabeth Bishop, a friendship that forms a central strand of the argument of *Becoming a Poet,* Merrill wrote:

First published in the *Kenyon Review*—New Series 19, no. 1 (winter 1997).

Amid the human welter what remained constant in the poets was their incapacity not to reach out for words, not to revise their songs. Their feelings, too, of mutual protectiveness. It is what happens when friends persist in seeing each other's best, and it is a note on which to let this book break off.

The man who wrote these valedictory words, and who has now himself been broken off, was surely thinking not only of the friendships between Lowell and Bishop or between Bishop and Marianne Moore—friendships Kalstone's study explores with characteristic curiosity, sympathy, and tact, as he follows the intertwined threads of art and life. As a close friend of Kalstone, Merrill must also have had in mind the "incapacity not to reach out for words" that marked his and DK's relationship. For, in addition to the afterword, Merrill wrote several poems to or about Kalstone over the course of his career. I'm thinking of the wonderful "Matinees" in *The Fire Screen* (1969); and Kalstone also figures slightly in the second and third volumes of the Sandover trilogy. But, as often happens with poetry, Kalstone's illness and death brought him into his own as a subject for Merrill's imagination. Two elegies for Kalstone, "Farewell Performance" and "Investiture at Cecconi's," as well as a mixed-genre piece, "Prose of Departure," all appear in Merrill's 1988 collection *The Inner Room*.

Unlike Kalstone, Merrill lived to complete his final book, *A Scattering of Salts* (1995). He did not, however, live quite long enough to see its publication; the book appeared just a month after his death. Around the same time that I was rereading Kalstone's books, then, I was also absorbed in this posthumous gift from a friend whose generosity it seemed even death couldn't hinder. And, as if the resulting cross-fertilization of reference and theme weren't enough, two other texts happened to come to hand at the same time. One I rediscovered on my bookshelf next to *Becoming a Poet:* it was the program of the memorial service held for Kalstone at the New York Public Library in September 1986, and it fortunately printed all the speakers' remarks in full. The other was a fine essay by Langdon Hammer in the spring 1995 issue of *Raritan,* entitled "Art and AIDS; or, How Will Culture Cure You?" Written before Merrill's death, the piece almost prefigures it.

The question that constitutes Hammer's title is a quotation from an elegy for Kalstone by Adrienne Rich. Kalstone is a central figure in Hammer's argument, for the essay tackles the question posed in its title by considering two elegies for Kalstone—the one by Rich and James Merrill's "Farewell Performance." Kalstone's love of the arts, acknowledged (as the memorial service program made clear and as I already knew) by all his friends, is central to both poems. In everything I was reading that spring, then, a heady mix of words and ideas combined with the fact of the recent death to connect art, friendship, and mortality.

A Scattering of Salts was in many ways a valedictory book. But the exact mode of valediction was clarified for me by the clutch of texts at hand. For example, more than one poem in *Salts* evokes places where the living and the dead, or the present and the past, can exchange glances for a moment. Such places are connected with performance, audience, friendship, and memory. The inevitable sadness of poems about the death of friends or about dead friends is lightened (salted?) by a wry sense of comedy. Helen Vendler observed years ago that Merrill's imagination, naturally light, airy, and darting, is pulled down by grief; and one can see the same dialectic of up and down playing itself out in these final pages.

In "The Ring Cycle" time is foreshortened for the speaker in the opera house in a manner reminiscent of another posthumous book, *Le Temps Retrouvé*. But the literary comparison that arises in the poem is far more down-home—not Proust but Thornton Wilder:

> Young love, moon-flooded hut, and the act ends.
> House lights. The matron on my left exclaims.
> We gasp and kiss. Our mothers were best friends.
> Now, old as mothers, here we sit. Too weird.
> That man across the aisle, with lambswool beard,
> Was once my classmate, or a year behind me.
> Alone, in black, in front of him, Maxine. . . .
> It's like the *Our Town* cemetery scene!

Maxine here is presumably the same person, Maxine Groffsky, who was a close friend of David Kalstone; she spoke at his memorial about their shared love of ballet. Maxine Groffsky, in turn, is mentioned in Merrill's tribute to Kalstone on the same occasion, when Merrill sketched for the mourners a little narrative of what became of Kalstone's ashes. Some were scattered in Long Island Sound, some outside Kalstone's beloved Venetian palazzo:

> . . . the little party went in a gondola to the Palazzo, and had it pause just below David's windows. Here Maxine took from her purse what she had brought, and emptied it into the black, starlit water of the Grand Canal.

The density of the cross-fertilization I've mentioned is demonstrated by the fact that Merrill's vignette—ashes into Grand Canal—was chosen by Richard Howard as the epigraph for *his* elegy to Kalstone, an elegy Hammer mentions but does not discuss in "How Will Culture Cure You?" Echo, reference, rumor, epigraph, memory—thus a culture is transmitted. The very word *transmission,* and by extension the notion of shared culture, is, in the age of AIDS, fraught with anxiety and threat, as Hammer's subtle and ingenious essay shows.

For Hammer culture (above all the performing arts but also poetry) is so closely associated with AIDS that it comes to be a perilously equivocal gift. For if culture can be, as Merrill phrases it in "Farewell Performance," "caught like a cold," so too can the mortal malady that occasioned Merrill's elegy for Kalstone (or Rich's elegy or Howard's or many others) in the first place. The love of a friend, the love of art, the love of art that one shares with a friend, which may even have brought the friends together in the first place, thus takes on a sinister subtext. Quoting "Farewell Performance," Hammer writes:

> Merrill finds himself desiring not simply to hail the dancers in their other world, but to join them there. Feigning a giddy naiveté, Merrill wonders aloud, "will a friend enroll us / one fine day?" The troupe Merrill speaks of is an elite company of artists, like that of *Five Temperaments,* as surely as it is the

spectral society of the AIDS dead. Heard as a question about sexually transmitted disease, the answer to Merrill's query is, Yes, indeed a friend may enroll you; maybe he already has. (*Raritan* 117)

The viral "culture" of AIDS and such human cultural manifestations as the love of ballet or opera are certainly alike in that both can be passed on. Still, what brought David Kalstone and Maxine Groffsky together in the first place—what enrolled *them* in the same troupe—was, as Groffsky tells us in her memorial tribute, ballet, not AIDS. Similarly, in Merrill's poem "The Ring Cycle" culture is above all the medium of human emotion. Maxine is "alone, in black" at the opera, like a widow, but she has still come to see "young love" and perhaps incidentally some old friends.

Culture, Hammer's essay concludes, cures no one. Indeed, music, ballet, and poetry keep no one alive—sick or well, HIV-positive or not. Nevertheless, just as Kalstone's subtle and empathetic analyses bring dead poets like Moore, Lowell, and Bishop back to a kind of life, so does Merrill's elegy bring Kalstone back to life, even though, paradoxically, it depicts him largely as ash. For in "Farewell Performance" Merrill avails himself to the full of the lyric privilege of apostrophe. The poet moves freely back and forth in time and space, fast-forwarding to the scene of Kalstone's ashes being scattered into Long Island Sound and back (or is it farther forward?) to a ballet performance. While acknowledging death, the poem always keeps the dead friend whom it addresses in the forefront of our minds. Hammer points out in "Can Culture Cure You?" that "aesthetic experience . . . break[s] down the boundary between people on stage and in the audience, between people who suffer and those who observe them." Aesthetic experience is also the place where the living can commune with the dead.

Reading again through the program of the memorial service for Kalstone reminded me that Elizabeth Bishop was an important, if disembodied, presence at that event. Like Merrill, Bishop was a poet Kalstone loved and wrote about; she is the central figure in *Becoming a Poet*. Cross-fertilization was at work here too, for the program pointed me to a place in Bishop's work where the sense of art as a breaker of boundaries, a joiner together of the living and the dead, is beautifully articulated.

In Kalstone's chapter on Bishop in *Five Temperaments* he discusses the sense in "Poem" of

> a shared pleasure in imaginative intensity, almost as if this remarkable writer were being surprised (you *hear* the surprise in her voice) at the power over loss and change which memory has given her writing.

The line Kalstone presumably has in mind when he refers to the audible surprise in Bishop's voice is "Heavens, I recognize the place, I know it!" as the realization dawns that the painting by the uncle she never knew is of a place she knows very well indeed. But there is another line, a little farther on in "Poem," which over the years has taken on an added resonance for me and which attests to a somewhat different kind of recognition: "I never knew him. We both knew this place."

The profound truth these nine simple words express is no less striking for not always necessarily being literally exact. To take a personal example, since I did have the good fortune to know David Kalstone slightly, it wouldn't be quite accurate for me to claim "I never knew him." Nevertheless, art, poetry—"this place"—is where he and I, or he and his many close friends, now meet; where loss, change, death itself, are powerless to separate us.

Bishop's luminous line was written in response to a painting, but it applies equally to a heartfelt response to a poem or indeed any work by an artist one never had the luck to know or could not, by the laws of chronology, possibly have known. For culture leaps boundaries of space and time. Such leaps can be thought of as infectious without the ominous connotation of illness and death, as laughter, or a taste for heroic couplets, kimonos, or Rhone wine can be passed on from one person to another—like a gift. Culture is given to someone. A work of art presupposes some kind of recipient, even if that person is removed in space and time, faceless, unknown, unimaginable.

And for the recipient, in turn, the gift may be obscure or delayed, hard to make out, hard to "get" in the sense both of receiving and understanding. As Bishop puts it in "Poem," this gift is "the little that we get for free, / the little of our earthly trust. / Not much."

Merrill's two elegies for Kalstone, both in sapphics, both collected in the same volume, feel like companion pieces. "Farewell Performance," the longer of the two and the one Hammer chooses to discuss, is the more obviously concerned with culture. "Investiture at Cecconi's," on the other hand, is more intimately involved with the nature of gifts. We have seen how the idea of any kind of transmission can be compromised, equivocal; and, indeed, illness frames "Investiture" even more directly than it does "Farewell Performance." The ominous phrase "after the diagnosis" occurs in its opening line and the phrase "sick, fearful" in its penultimate line. Further, the kimono—"cool silk in grave white folds—Oriental mourning—" (18) is, even apart from the pun on *grave*, doubly eerie. The kimono suggests both proleptic mourning for the dying friend who has occasioned this sad gift and also (a reading for which I am indebted to Hammer's essay) contagion. "Up my own arms glistening sleeves are drawn"; the speaker too must now don the special gown that belongs not only to the mourner but to the patient, hospitalized, perhaps quarantined.

The double-edged nature of this dream gift becomes unmistakable by the final stanza of "Investiture," where the speaker is equally overwhelmed by the splendor of the gift and by the circumstances under which it has been given:

> *Thank your friend,* she cackles, *the Professore!*
> Wonderstruck, I sway, like a tree of tears. You—
> miles away, sick, fearful—have yet arranged this
> heartstopping present.

In his discussion of Merrill's work in *Five Temperaments* Kalstone taught us twenty years ago to be on the alert for double meanings in Merrill's use of language. So *heartstopping:* incredible, awe-inspiring; also death-dealing. *Present* too asks to be taken more than one way. *Present* denotes not only gift but also the verb tense associated with one's current state—now, here, this. Thus, "miles away, sick, fearful," the dying man has nevertheless managed to effect one last passionate connection. He has given the speaker a particular kind of present in more ways than one.

The pervasive suggestion of disease is misunderstood if it prevents us from reading "Investiture" as a poem of love, gratitude, and grief. Merrill accurately captures the economy of dreams; mourning here is inseparable from, indeed embodied in, the gift. The point is clear: presents given by one friend to another sooner or later become gifts given to the living by the dead. Presently (heartstopping present!) the living die too; but not, if they are artists, without having passed on their gifts to still others, in an endless reticulation of connections, a cloud of cross-fertilization.

In "Investiture" there seems to be no question of refusing the kimono once it has been recognized, even though this gift isn't what the dreamer thought he was after at the tailor's shop ("I wanted evening / clothes for the new year"). But culture is an altogether more portable offering than even a silk kimono—one that can be given away and kept at the same time. Culture spread through friendship is all the richer for being shared; yet mortality ordains that in the course of time we must not invest but divest.

Divestment, a lightening of cargo, is important in Merrill's work at least as early as "Santorini: Stopping the Leak," collected in *Late Settings* (1985):

> We must be light, light-footed, light of soul,
> Quick to let go, to tighten by a notch
> The broad, star-studded belt Earth wears to feel
> Hungers less mortal for a vanished whole . . .
> And if (weeks later, Athens) life still weighs
> Too heavily, why, leave the bulk behind. . . .

A more essential as well as more drastic lightening, amounting not to divestment but to transformation, occurs in Merrill's memoir, *A Different Person,* in a context that is now uncannily familiar to me. Mourning his friend Hans Lodeizen's premature death, Merrill receives Hans's posthumous book of poems. Just how does the departed person inhere in the pages?

> Between these ounces of paper and print he had become . . .
> and the person I'd known and loved lay all the difference in the
> world. I glimpsed . . . the degree to which I was consenting to
> the transformation my friend had already . . . undergone . . .
> wouldn't I too turn, word by word, page by page, into books on
> a shelf?

Sometimes one is vouchsafed the privilege of catching Merrill in the act, word by word, of turning life into literature, or, as Bishop puts it in "Poem," of compressing life even as it is lived into "the memory of it." For in letters and postcards, the occasional prose of a life filled with friends, Merrill often tested out images that would later find more public homes in the poems.

A glimpse of this process is afforded if we compare "Farewell Performance" to Merrill's memorial tribute to Kalstone. The passage from the tribute I quoted earlier shows us Maxine Groffsky emptying a vial into the Grand Canal. Merrill also describes the scattering of Kalstone's ashes in Stonington:

> It was a calm, brilliant day. Peter held on to a mooring, while I
> emptied the box underwater. In the sunlit current the white
> gravel of our friend fanned out, revolving once as if part of a
> dance, and was gone. So, for the time being, were the dread
> and sorrow with which that day had begun.

In "Farewell Performance" the little scene is theatricalized. Both the title and the guiding trope of the poem gain an eerie force if we realize that the final performance in question is not only one at the New York City Ballet; it is Kalstone's own posthumous dance step underwater:

> this is what we paddled a neighbour's dinghy
> out to scatter—Peter who grasped the buoy,
> I who held the box underwater, freeing
> all it contained. Past

> sunny, fluent soundings that gruel of selfhood
> taking manlike shape for one last jeté on
> ghostly—wait, ah!—point into darkness vanished.
> High up, a gull's wings
>
> clapped. The house lights (always supposing, caro,
> Earth remains your house) at their brightest set the
> scene for good . . .

(17–20)

"Life and memory of it" interact more wryly in another poem to a departed friend—Elizabeth Bishop herself. Judging by its title, "Overdue Pilgrimage to Nova Scotia," in *A Scattering of Salts,* is a poem its author felt he should have written sooner. But the poem may have taken Merrill so long after Bishop's death in 1979 to write precisely because it wasn't until he had visited the village that was the scene of Bishop's earliest memories, and some of her best work, that he could fully feel "we both knew this place." (The elegies for Kalstone, whom Merrill saw constantly in New York, Venice, and Stonington, presented no such challenge.)

This is not to imply that Merrill "never knew" Elizabeth Bishop. On the contrary, the fact that the two poets were close friends—he visited her in Brazil; they corresponded for years—was exactly what made his elegy for her shamefully "overdue." Nevertheless, despite Bishop's and Merrill's friendship, "Overdue Pilgrimage" beautifully fulfills Bishop's "never knew / both knew" formulation. For, as if on cue, a figure who, never having known Bishop, knows the village well turns up at the end of the first stanza. Can't we hear an echo of "Poem"?

> the fair, soft-spoken girl who shows us through.
> Although till now she hasn't heard of you
> She knows these things you would have known by heart
> And we, by knowing you by heart, foreknew.

The end of "Overdue Pilgrimage" finds Merrill and his traveling companion sitting in their car as the suds from a car wash cascade over the vehicle. To use Helen Vendler's term for a mode common in late Merrill, this scene is a kind of reprise of the dinghy scene in "Farewell Performance." The speaker and a companion (Peter Hooten, the same person in both cases) sit in a vehicle surrounded by water, drawn there by the felt presence of and a sense of obligation to a dead friend. But there's an important difference. In "Overdue Pilgrimage" each echoed element of the scene in "Farewell Performance" feels parodic. Instead of dinghy on the brilliant Sound, we now have an enclosed car in a car wash—and this in a poem that has just touched upon the destruction of nature, throughout Bishop's beloved Northeast, by acid rain. The atmosphere cannot be cleansed, even if cars can. And how ironically appropriate for a tribute to Bishop, the author of a poem entitled "Filling Station," that the pilgrims in their car have found one:

> What tribute could you hear
> Without dismay? Well, facing where you lived
> Somebody's been inspired (*can* he have read
> "Filling Station"?) to put pumps, a sign:
> ESSO—what else! We filled up at the shrine.

Unscathed by the man-made cascade of lather, the friends sit in the equivocal shelter of a car—the car that soon, at the end of the poem, will be their means of escape. At this point the tone of parody shifts disconcertingly from the car wash—an easy target, after all—to the language-driven creatures inside the car. It's also disconcerting that Bishop herself has apparently been rinsed from the stanza:

> So here we sit in the car-wash, snug and dry
> As the pent-up fury of the storm hits: streaming,
> Foaming "emotions"—impersonal, cathartic,
> Closer to both art and what we are
> Than the gush of nothings one outpours to people
> On the correspondence side of bay and steeple
> Whose dazzling whites we'll never see again,
> Or failed to see in the first place. Still, as the last
> Suds glide, slow protozoa, down the pane,
> We're off—Excuse our dust! With warm regards,
> Gathering phrases for tomorrow's cards.

That "gush of nothings" has an undeniable astringency. But, weary though Merrill may have grown, the outpouring is his lifelong poetic impulse and habit—both a gesture of friendship and a step on the way to turning life into literature. The "dazzling whites of bay and steeple" won't reappear in this life; indeed, he may have "failed to see [them] in the first place." But here they are, captured on paper—on a card purchased for the express purpose of communicating. Those "dazzling whites" have a double antecedent. They obviously refer to bay and steeple, that is, the photos of Nova Scotia depicted on the cards. But the "correspondence side" of those cards is also white—until the poet writes on it.

There's another dimension to this outpouring. Although the elegist will "never see again" Elizabeth Bishop or David Kalstone, he can still travel on their account—both "Farewell Performance" and "Overdue Pilgrimage" are accounts of errands of affection—and can still address the resulting poems (like the tourist's postcards) to them. Finally, if Merrill sounds impatient with a lifetime's "gush of nothings," his sharpness is only the other side of the coin from the tender ruefulness with which he noted (in the passage to his afterword to *Becoming a Poet* that we've already seen) that "amid the human welter what remained constant in the poets was their incapacity not to reach out for words."

"Impersonal and cathartic" as a Greek tragedy, the suds cleanse the car window. With their vision thus refreshed, the pilgrims set forth once more on their quest for "phrases for tomorrow's cards," driven, as Merrill so well knows is the way of poets, by just that incapacity not to reach out for words.

I was one of the many friends to whom Merrill wrote a postcard setting the scene of his final weeks in Tucson. And, while I'm reluctant to think of that cherished last card from my friend as a gush or even a trickle of nothing, there's no doubt at all that Merrill used just such cards to gather "phrases for tomorrow's" *poems*. He could please his friends and attend to his art at the same time.

The formula "I never knew him. We both knew this place" undergoes yet another metamorphosis here: the recipient of the card (in this case me) knows the person but not the place, so, like a courteous host, Merrill shows me around the property in a cameo tour that (like so much in *A Scattering of Salts*) is both charming and unnerving:

> We've been here a week and love it. House of cinematic spaciousness, pool of koi among the daffodils, sun pouring in. "Fascinating new friends," as the old Cunard brochures used to say. Coyotes too, I'm afraid, licking their chops at the prospect of a small overprivileged unguarded dog.

Those unnamed, generic-sounding friends; the reference to Cunard brochures—are these examples of the gush of nothings Merrill seems to dismiss in "Overdue Pilgrimage"? To me they set the human scene and scale with the precision Merrill so admired in his friend Elizabeth Bishop's work, with the difference that his more gregarious nature populates even a miniature evocation of place with companions who are economically characterized.

Yet the "fascinating new friends" also seem faintly unreal, a period piece—at most, a backdrop to the central concern of the card. Or rather (for I am now confusing "life and the memory of it," card and poem) the central concern of Merrill's last completed and posthumously published poem "Koi," which, like the card, was written in Tucson sometime around mid-January 1995, weeks before Merrill's death. Although the friends and the world of Cunard liners have vanished from "Koi," the poem functions rather as the card did. This time not fascinating new friends but an unusual Arizona snowstorm provides a distraction, but, when it clears away, something much more frightening becomes apparent—something the word *resumes* tells us was there all along:

> the terrain resumes its menace.
> Coyotes patrol it, watchful for a small
> Privileged dog to steal! Premonitions! Whole nights
> Preliving the yelp of pain and disbelief
>
> As we helplessly watch our Cosmo borne struggling off.

A hovering sense of imminent violation and separation, of being dragged off and devoured, cohabits here with the sunlit pool. "Koi" ends with comic relief, with the delicious pun "*Carpe diem*" and the slapstick of our "Lindbergh puppy" (the "small overprivileged unguarded dog" of the card) falling not into a coyote's jaws but into the pool. But the poignancy remains—as do the multiple reticulations of the poet's art, even in apparently casual details. For, if "Lindbergh" calls up the overprivileged child's fantasies in "Days of 1935," the pool is perhaps the final version of Long Island Sound where Kalstone's ashes were scattered, or the Grand Canal where Maxine emptied the vial, or even the suds gliding down the windowpane in "Overdue Pilgrimage." One thinks too of the broken mirror and the watered plant at the end of *Scripts for the Pageant*. Every one of these valedictory occasions involves two sets of friends, the present and the absent or the living and the dead. The poet bids farewell to one set of friends and reports on the farewell to another set. Even those fascinating new friends of that final postcard are a potential audience for the forthcoming farewell surely already outlined in Merrill's imagination—the farewell to Tucson, say, or (a worst-case scenario) a farewell to Cosmo. Merrill didn't envision the last cards and poems as his own farewell—or did he? "Wouldn't I too turn, word by word, page by page, into books on a shelf?"

To be a friend, in our foreshortened mortal world, is to be obligated to say good-bye. Culture doesn't make good-byes necessary; life and death do that. But it does make them beautiful.

From Stage Set to Heirloom

Greece in the Work of James Merrill

In April 1996, when the Hellenic Cultural Foundation of New York City mounted a memorial exhibition on the subject of James Merrill in Greece, I was asked to talk about any aspect of the poet's work that related to Greece or Hellenism. My solution was to assemble a little showcase, a mini-anthology of subthemes to introduce some of the patterns and preoccupations that recur in the rich variety of poems Merrill wrote in and about Greece. Some poems, for example, use Greece as a backdrop or stage set; others locate Greece or Greekness in a particular person; some are love poems that might be set anywhere (or might they?); and some poems see the country as a gift or heirloom, a keepsake to be both cherished and handed on.

At the time, I thought the Greek language itself was one more category or theme among others. But rereading Merrill's work since 1996 has changed my mind. It now seems to me that, rather than being one possible way of grasping or troping Greece, the Greek language is the principal source and form of much of the enchantment and glamor that energize what Merrill wrote in Greece. So, before touching upon the other forms Greece and Hellenism take in the work, it's worth considering first Merrill's relation to Greek over the years. The subject is one that crops up time and again outside the poetry—in interviews, in Merrill's memoir, and in his essay on Cavafy. Interviewers' questions may not always address the Greek language, but, as I came to see, Merrill's answers often do.

From *Arion* 4, no. 1 (spring 1999).

Why, he was often asked, did you go to Greece and spend so much time there? Of course, people's motives are both mixed and submerged; any one explanation is likely to be incomplete and overdetermined at once. Merrill was gracious, expansive, and also elusive when responding to interviewers' questions about what Greece meant to him. But it's consistently striking that, by the poet's own account, the beauty of the landscape and the character of the people were secondary for him to the vividness of the language he heard being spoken—its allure, its drama, its unintelligibility. In a 1972 interview Merrill told David Kalstone that the poet is "a man choosing the words he lives by." What Greece meant to Merrill was inseparable from what Greek meant to him.

In his 1993 memoir, *A Different Person*, Merrill recalls his impressions of Athens when he first visited the city in 1950:

> Unlike Paris, where the most banal sidewalk set me quivering because Debussy or Wilde or Cocteau might have set foot on it, Greece and all its splendors would have to work long and hard, like Greek immigrants in the slums of New York, to earn their keep in my blocked imagination . . . Having taken some ancient Greek at college, I could transliterate the billboards and street signs. But the great, the single luxury now freely available in this society shattered not only by the German and Italian occupations but by the civil war . . . was talk, and this I could not share. Everybody else, from teenaged surrealist to white-haired bootblack, was engaged in dialogue, in fluent speech and vehement gesture. New ideas glowed with the lighting of a fresh cigarette . . .

When did Merrill learn enough Greek to do more than transliterate billboards? According to Stephen Yenser, very promptly:

> Like the main figure in his poem "The Friend of the Fourth Decade," perhaps, he wanted to go to a country in whose language he knew "barely enough to ask for food and love." But James had studied ancient Greek at Amherst, and he must have begun learning demotic Greek even before he and David Jackson bought a house there. When I first visited him in Athens— in 1971—he was apologetic about his Greek, and even in years

to come he never claimed fluency, saying always that he had no vocabulary for "abstractions." But in all of the time I spent with him in Athens, I never saw him at a loss, whether he was talking to Greek friends or Greek bureaucrats. Indeed, he wrote a few poems in Greek, and letters to friends in Greek. His simplification of things was also an immense complication. (Talk given at the Hellenic Cultural Foundation Merrill exhibit, April 1996)

I met Merrill in Athens in 1969, and my experience confirms Yenser's description. The initial unintelligibility of spoken Greek had been replaced by enough comprehension to make the "fluent speech" of the people he met less opaque—though still sufficiently foreign to be alluring. In 1968 Merrill told the interviewer Ashley Brown:

> Since I've been living in Greece I've found myself thinking a lot about human behavior. It's because of the language barrier— when you can't ascertain the full range of people's motives and feelings, they are simplified in a sense . . . I think I like either those people who completely understand whatever I say—at all levels—or those who understand hardly any of it, for whom I am simplified into a dream-figure, as they no doubt are for me. Understanding has more than one face.

These thoughts arose in the context not of Merrill's sojourns in Greece but of the long ballad "The Summer People," which he was working on at the time (it was published in *The Fire Screen*, 1969)—a poem that ponders human behavior in Stonington, Connecticut. The poem also considers the generic confines of the ballad form: "Figures in a ballad / Lend themselves to acts / Tragical and simple. / A bride weeps. A tree cracks." But perhaps such simplicity was made more available to Merrill by the half of each year he was then spending in Greece, where the language barrier (such as it was) facilitated simplification "into a dream-figure." Later, in *The Book of Ephraim*, mentioning the lost novel, Merrill refers again to simplified characters, "the kinds of being we recall from Grimm, / Jung, Verdi, and the commedia dell'arte." Depicting such characters, though, turned out to be "beyond me."

Simplification never came naturally to Merrill—precisely the point of Yenser's paradoxical statement that the poet's "simplification of things was also an immense complication." But in the face of his natural bent toward complexity, Merrill was drawn toward its opposite. The European tour described in *A Different Person* coincided with a period of youthful writer's block: how to move past the ornate style of the poems he had already written? The vivid, gestural language the young man heard in Athens "answered to the kind of poem I hoped to write." And it may well be that the fairy-tale feeling of some of the work in *The Fire Screen* or *Braving the Elements*—I'm thinking of poems like "The Summer People" and "Days of 1935"—was made possible by the fairy-tale feeling of life as lived partly in another language.

Here, for example, describing a 1960 visit to Patmos, Merrill evokes his hosts' formulaic courtesy with its echoes of epic convention—the forerunner of fairy tales, simplified and smoothed by generations ("licked . . . by mild old tongues," *Ephraim*): "The household . . . has a beautiful daughter. Next morning as I return, toothbrush in hand and towel round neck, from a distant washroom, she and an older sister ask the usual question. Who art thou, Stranger, and what brings thee hither?"

That such a question can be asked unselfconsciously not only opens out possibilities for Merrill's own work; it also enables him to perceive Greece as a cultural continuum, so that Homer, Cavafy, and contemporary poets can be seen to be executing the same gesture. The following passage, from Merrill's splendid 1975 essay on Cavafy, sheds light on a poem like "Days of 1964" as well as on the Alexandrian poet:

> The gods appeared to characters in Homer disguised as a mortal friend or stranger. Put in terms acceptable nowadays, that was a stylized handling of those moments familiar to us all when the stranger's idle word or the friend's sudden presence happens to strike deeply into our spirits . . . The unity of divine and human, or past and present, is as real to [Cavafy] as their disparity. Between the poor, unlettered, present-day young men and the well-to-do, educated ones in his historical

poems . . . there is an unbroken bond of type and disposition . . . This bond is at the marrow of Cavafy's feeling. It reflects his situation as a Greek, *the dynamics of his language,* indeed the whole legacy of Hellenism. (My italics.)

The human feeling and the historical situation are jointly expressed in language. In another passage from the Cavafy essay, when Merrill refers to "the ancient glory," he is thinking not of a young man's beauty or the ruins of a temple so much as of the durable and resilient Greek language:

> while the ancient glory may have grown dim and prosaic, many forms of it are still intact. . . . The language survives the reversals of faith and empire, and sharpens the dull wits of the barbarian. The glory dwindles and persists.

Part of the story of Merrill and Greek, then, is this luminous synchronicity, this long vista afforded more by the continuity of the Greek language than by the beauty of the place or the architecture. But life has to be lived in the present. Perhaps Merrill's linguistic talent made him too quick a study for his own comfort. Once he was steeped in this new place and particularly language, they ceased to be new; with Proustian inevitability they became familiar, then transparent, then invisible. It was at this point that the formerly strange new world of Greece and Greek gave way, in the poet's imagination, to the much more uncanny new world (also complete with the fresh dramatis personae of the Ouija board). One common denominator was the lure of the challenge. Asked by J. D. McClatchy, in a 1982 interview in the *Paris Review,* what it was he had originally found in Greece, Merrill replied with rueful nostalgia:

> Things that have mostly disappeared, I'm afraid. The dazzling air, the drowsy waterfronts. Our own ignorance, even: a language we didn't understand two words of at first. That was a holiday! You could imagine that others were saying extraordinarily fascinating things—the point was to invent, if not what they were saying, at least its implications, its overtones.

There's an echo here (both verbal resemblance and parallel thought) of Merrill's poem "Matinees," in which being enamored of opera teaches the child to invent his own dramas: "The point thereafter was to arrange for one's / Own chills and fevers, passions and betrayals, / Chiefly in order to make song of them." The songs are made; the knowledge of the art form (or language) is gained; but perhaps the passion wanes. At any rate, as far as Greek was concerned, Merrill's holiday of ignorance was an evanescent one. After a while it's no longer possible to delude oneself into imagining that "others were saying extraordinarily fascinating things." It is as if a child finally realizes how boring the grownups are; comprehension becomes lackluster and must give way to invention.

The punningly titled poem "To My Greek," which braids allegory, metamorphosis, and eros in a scene of domestic comedy, suggests the progress of Merrill's knowledge of the tongue (or of a person who speaks it) together with the way his feelings change. Even excerpted, the poem shows some of what we've already seen: Merrill's self-proclaimed weak vocabulary for abstractions; the attraction and exasperation of being a pupil again; the way a landscape turns out to be a blank page or a world of words. The sketched scene of nude swimming at the end is a bold metaphor for exploring the depths both of a language and of a heart. After all, Merrill's 1971 collection, much of it written in Greece, was entitled *Braving the Elements*.

To My Greek

Dear nut
Uncrackable by nuance or debate,
Eat with your fingers, wear your bloomers to bed,

Under my skin stay nude. Let past and future

Perish upon our lips, ocean inherit
Those paper millions. Let there be no word
For justice, grief, convention; you be convention—
Goods, bads, kaló-kakó, cockatoo-raucous

Coastline of white printless coves

Already strewn with offbeat echolalia.
Forbidden Salt Kiss Wardrobe Foot Cloud Peach
—Name it, my chin drips sugar. Radiant dumbbell, each

Noon's menus and small-talk leave you

Likelier, each sunset yawned away,
Hair in eyes, head bent above the strummed
Lexicon, gets by heart about to fail
This or that novel mode of being together
Without conjunctions . . .

. . . .

Having chosen the way of little knowledge,

Trusted each to use the other
Kindly except in moments of gross need,
Come put the verb-wheel down
And kiss my mouth despite the foot in it.

Let schoolboys brave her shallows. Sheer

Lilting azure float them well above
Those depths the surfacer
Lives, when he does, alone to sound and sound.

The barest word be what I say in you.

For all its relaxed wit "To My Greek" is a remarkably con-
densed evocation of a love affair with a language. Since one of
Merrill's great subjects is love, the poem has a programmatic
force; it feels more than merely occasional. The other pro-
grammatic passage about language I think of in Merrill can
also be applied to Greek, but more than "To My Greek" it
transcends the particular situation—or rather is designed to
apply to a wide variety of situations. From *The Book of Ephraim:*

> Hadn't—from books, from living—
> The profusion dawned on us, of "languages"
> Any one of which, to who could read it,
> Lit up the system it conceived?—bird-flight,
> Hallucinogen, chorale and horoscope:
> Each its own world, hypnotic, many-sided
> Facet of the universal gem.

Let's use the image of the gem to move from Merrill's uses of the Greek language to a quick survey of some of the other ways Greece or Greekness appears in the poetry. Key to the image of the jewel is its many-facetedness; it can't be perceived from one aspect alone. In this the "universal gem" of the world is like Lambert Strether's awed sense of Paris in *The Ambassadors:*

> It hung before him this morning . . . like some huge iridescent object, a jewel brilliant and hard, in which parts were not to be discriminated nor differences comfortably marked. It twinkled and trembled and melted together; and what seemed all surface one moment seemed all depth the next.

Just such a disconcerting alternation of foreground and background is markedly the case with much of Merrill's work, and nowhere more so than in the poems that use Greece as a setting. Often the scene appears secondary to the human drama enacted there, but take away the Greek setting and in many cases the essence of the poem would leak away. The poems quoted here are more ambitious and complex than mere snapshots of places yet are also precisely that—vividly detailed pictures of a harbor, a bar, a neighborhood at Christmas. Examples could be multiplied; I limit myself to five. In "Chimes for Yahya" (1976) the scene (Merrill's Lycabettos neighborhood on Christmas morning) serves as prologue to the memory of a dead friend. The recalled story of Merrill's youthful visit to Yahya takes up most of the poem, but the opening passage of "Chimes" is an accurate account of the traditional Greek children's visits on Christmas morning, of Merrill's front door with its "frosted glass," and the scene downtown. What might look like local color is the surface of the present, which at the end of the passage opens out to reveal the past, neatly illustrating Henry James's formulation that "what seemed all surface one moment seemed all depth the next."

Chimes for Yahya

Imperiously ringing, Νά τά πούμε;
("Shall we tell it?") two dressy little girls inquire.

They mean some chanted verse to do with Christmas
Which big homemade iron triangles
Drown out and a least coin silences
But oh hell not at seven in the morning
If you please! and SLAM the frosted glass
Spares me their tidings and themselves
Further inspection of the foreigner
Grizzled and growling in his flannel robe.
All day children will be prowling loose
Eager to tell, tell, tell what the angel said.
So, having gagged the mechanism with a towel,
Washed hands and face, put on the kettle—
But bells keep ringing in my head.
Downhill too, where priests pace in black dresses,
Chignons and hats, like Chekhov's governesses,
Their toy church on a whole block of bare earth
In central Athens (what it must be worth!)
Clangs like a locomotive—well, good lord,
Why not? Tomorrow's Christmas. All aboard.

A short poem from 1985, "The Metro," memorializes a now
defunct bar beneath Omonia Square in downtown Athens:

One level below street, an airless tank—
We'd go there evenings, watch through glass the world
Eddy by, winking, casting up
Such gorgeous flotsam that hearts leapt, or sank.

Over the bar, in polychrome relief,
A jungle idyll: tiger, water hole,
Mate lolling on her branch, aperitif-
Green eyes aglare. We also lolled and drank,

Joking with scarface Kosta, destitute
Sotiri, Plato in his new striped suit . . .
Those tigers are no more now. The bar's gone,
And in its place, O memory! a bank.

A benign jungle or waterhole, a place for cruising and hunt-
ing not tigers but boys in striped suits, has given way to a place
of much more impersonal exchange—a bank. The little poem
presages, probably unintentionally, the globalization that has

made neighborhoods all over the world less eccentric, more stereotyped. More to the point, it also recalls a little Cavafy poem, "In the Same Space":

> The setting of houses, cafes, the neighborhood
> that I've seen and walked through years on end:
>
> I created you while I was happy, while I was sad,
> with so many incidents, so many details.
>
> And for me, the whole of you has been transformed
>   into feeling.
>
> (Trans. Edmund Keeley)

The note struck here is elegiac in a different way from "The Metro," but both poems record the transforming work of time and memory on the human scale of a neighborhood. Cavafy's untranslatable verb αισθήματοιηθηκες, which applies to most of Merrill's Greek poems, is another example of the confusing alteration of surface and depth. The Metro bar too has been changed from one kind of place to another while simultaneously remaining preserved in memory.

In "Samos," the canzone in *Mirabell*, Merrill sketches the harbor at Vathy on the island of Samos; in "Yannina" he depicts the marketplace in that sleepy town. These passages are not only brief but relatively minor in the larger scheme of each poem. Yet both are all the more vivid because the poems they inhabit pass quickly on to bigger matters; neither insists on the picturesqueness of the scene, but both embody it, letting the reader choose whether or not to linger.

> Here we were. The twins of Sea and land,
> Up and about for hours—hues, cries, scents—
> Had placed at eye level a single light
> Croissant: the harbor glazed with warm pink light.
>
> ("Samos")

> Somnambulists along the promenade
> Have set up booths, their dreams:
> Carpets, jewelry, kitchenware, halvah, shoes.

From a loudspeaker passionate lament
Mingles with the penny jungle's roars and screams.
Tonight in the magician's tent
Next door a woman will be sawed in two,
But right now she's asleep, as who is not, as who . . .

                                                    ("Yannina")

A final example of Merrill's use of Greece as setting calls to
mind the notion of simplification. If the foreignness of the
Greek language simplified speakers into dream-figures, here a
generic setting at once foreign and deeply familiar—Athens
revisited—simplifies (or complicates) the speaker into a char-
acter onstage. The poem here is "Nine Lives," published in
Merrill's posthumous *A Scattering of Salts*. Visiting Athens
again, staying in his old house, he sees this stay—or this life—
as nonetheless real for being essentially theatrical.

The ancient comic theater had it right:
A shuttered house, a street or square, a tree
Collect, life after life, the energy
To flood what happens in their shade with light.
A house in Athens does the trick for me—
Thrilling to find oneself again on stage,
In character, at this untender age.

The streamlined stylization suggested by this passage leads
to another facet of Merrill's Greek poems. It might be called
reduction or distillation; one could also use the title of *Braving
the Elements* and call it elemental. Remember the last line of
"To My Greek," "the barest word be what I say in you." This
stripped-down simplification should already be familiar, but in
some of Merrill's Greek work the simplifying process is ap-
plied to larger and more abstract categories than people or a
language. In the 1965 novel *The (Diblos) Notebook* climate and
landscape combine with language to form the elements of
nothing less than a new self:

Thanks, say, to little more than a ray of sun entering the honey-
cells of marble, I felt my whole person cleansed and restored.

My skin turned olive brown. The Latinate vocabulary to which I leaned when thinking or speaking in English gave way to authentic, simple forms: rock, sea, sun, wine, goat, sky [compare "Forbidden Salt Kiss Wardrobe Foot Cloud Peach"]. That the land was poor & stony, that the modern language had been, like the wine, thinned and impregnated with resin, made no difference. I myself felt poor & pungent enough to take my place among the marble rubble, the lizard, spine plants, clouds of dust and sparkle of salt water—all these things on which the Greek sun dotes & which are intolerable without it.

We would be wrong to discount the irony here. The callow narrator of *The (Diblos) Notebook,* himself a fledging author, half-knowingly exemplifies such banal responses as the delusion that Greek words are "simple, authentic forms." The poem "After Greece" deploys this "simple" new idiom (light, oil, stones, moon, columns) to create a deceptively legible landscape of "old ideas / Found lying open to the elements." The bareness, simplicity, directness, and so forth prove illusory; back in America the poem's speaker dreams that the caryatids on the Erechtheum have been transposed into his great-great grandmother.

"Another August" (1969) takes a disenchanted look at repetition, the expected, the generic—perhaps things Greece had begun to seem to Merrill. (Even the title seems to shrug wearily; and it's noteworthy that the poem begins as prose before picking up rhythm and intensity.) Does familiarity falsify? The poem's refusal to give a simple answer is a clue that Merrill himself in all his percipience and ambivalence is the speaker, rather than some imagined young novelist. Despite its greater astringency, "Another August," particularly its "Envoi for S.," reads like a forerunner of "Nine Lives": in both, the setting allows (necessitates?) the playing of a role.

Another August

Pines. The white, ochre-pocked houses. Sky unflawed. Upon so much former strangeness a calm settles, glaze of custom to be neither shattered nor shattered by. Home. Home at last.

Years past—blind, tattering
wind, hall, tears—my head was in those clouds
that now are dark pearl in my head.
Open the shutters. Let variation
abandon the swallows one by one.
How many summer dusks were needed
to make that single skimming form!
The very firefly kindles to its type.
Here is each evening's lesson. First
the hour, the setting. Only then
the human being, his white shirtsleeve
chalked among treetrunks, round a waist,
or lifted in an entrance. Look for him.
Be him.

Envoi for S.

Whom you saw mannerless and dull of heart,
Easy to fool, impossible to hurt,
I wore that fiction like a fine white shirt
And asked no favor but to play the part.

"S.," Merrill's lover, Stratos Mouflouzelis, figures in many of
the Greek poems. Some of these are love poems. "Days of
1964" is too long to quote, but the motifs of god in disguise,
of depth versus surface, and of Greece as stage set all apply
to that beautiful poem. Less well-known is the lyric gem
"Last Words," a poem that in expressing love also bids fare-
well to the protean transformations of the lover even as it
celebrates them.

My life, your light green eyes
Have lit on me with joy.
There's nothing I don't know
Or shall not know again,
Over and over again.
It's noon, it's dawn, it's night,
I am the dog that dies
In the deep street of Troy
Tomorrow, long ago—
Part of me brims with pain,

Becomes the stinging flies,
The bent head of the boy.
Part looks into your light
And lives to tell you so.

One more transformation: on display at the Hellenic Cultural Foundation's exhibit on Merrill, and reproduced in the exhibit's catalog, is the poet's translation into Greek of "Last Words," presumably for the benefit of Strato.

In "Strato in Plaster" (1972) Strato is not the beloved addressed by the poem but a character in a bittersweet scene. Heavier, older, he turns up at Merrill's door, his broken arm in a cast. Life meets art head on:

> Here at hand is a postcard Chester sent
> Of the Apollo at Olympia,
> Its message *Strato as he used to be.*
> Joy breeds in the beautiful blind gaze,
> The marble mouth and breastbone. I look hard
> At both the god and him. (He loves attention
> Like gods and children, and he lifts his glass.)
> Those extra kilos, that mustache,
> Lies found out and letters left unanswered
> Just won't do. It makes him burst out laughing,
> Curiously happy, flecked with foam.

The Greek workman as a living Apollo may be Chester Kallman's idea, but it is also pure Cavafy, as Merrill knew. The Alexandrian poet wrote in "Days of 1909, '10 and '11":

> I ask myself if the great Alexandria
> of ancient times could boast of a boy
> more exquisite, more perfect—
> thoroughly neglected though he was;
> that is, we don't have a statue or painting of him;
> thrust into that poor ironmonger's shop,
> overworked, harassed, given to cheap debauchery,
> he was soon used up.
>
> (Trans. Edmund Keeley)

Because of the dramatically clustering nature of Merrill's imagination, this incident, poignant and evocative in itself, is also one of a series of encounters in a continuing relationship—one scene among many in the ongoing drama of lives played out against the complicatedly simple backdrop of the house in Athens.

Merrill also has at least two dramatic monologues spoken in the voices of the young men for whom the poems are named. These poems achieve the remarkable effect of being at once in Merrill's fluent and elegant English and in demotic Greek; for example, the expression "death took my father" in the next poem is a literal translation of a common way of saying someone has died. In sticking close to what the people in question really said, these poems, like speeches in a good play, also convey the character of the speakers. I never knew Kostas Tympakianakis, but "Manos Karastefanis" reads like a composite of things this serious, wistful young athlete might well have said during a succession of conversations. The poem captures his gentle, puzzled manner.

Death took my father.
The same year (I was twelve)
Thanási's mother taught me
Heaven and hell.

None of my army buddies
Called me by name—
Just "Styles" or "Fashion Plate."
One friend I had, my body,

And, evenings at the gym
Contending with another,
Used it to isolate
Myself from him.

The doctor saved my knee.
You came to the clinic
Bringing *War and Peace*,
Better than any movie.

Why are you smiling?
I fought fair, I fought well,
Not hurting my opponent,
To win this black belt.

Why are you silent?
I've brought you a white cheese
From my island, and the sea's
Voice in a shell.

It would be interesting to see a poem like this translated into Greek; it is in itself a kind of translation from Greek. Few if any of Cavafy's poems let the young men in them speak, but Merrill welcomes the challenge.

A final theme in Merrill's Greek poems to be considered here is that of the heirloom, keepsake, or gift—something to be acquired or given and cherished but then passed on. (This theme has sprung into focus since Merrill's death; his great generosity in art and in life seemed to circumvent mortality precisely by passing on his riches.) The poems sometimes touch upon moments of taking, sometimes of giving up. In the brief "More Enterprise" a local gesture becomes an acquired characteristic.

A sideways flicker, half headshake of doubt
Meaning, confusingly, assent—fills out
The scant wardrobe of gesture I still use.
It clings by habit now. The old strait swank
I came in struts the town on local heirs.
Koula's nephew has the suit she shrank,
Andreas coveted my Roman shoes. . . .
Into the grave I'll wear that Yes of theirs.

The new gesture—a Greek version of our nod for yes—functions here as a kind of exchange for the largess Merrill has himself distributed. Is it significant that this gesture of assent, more incorporeal than shoes or a suit, will also last longer? "Santorini: Stopping the Leak," a poem occasioned by a trip to that island during one of Merrill's last stays in Greece, ponders a medley of divestments, a variety of belt-tightenings including something as simple as giving M. (Manos Karastefanis) a bed:

> We must be light, light-footed, light of soul,
> Quick to let go, to tighten by a notch
> The broad, star-studded belt Earth wears, to feel
> Hungers less mortal for a vanished whole.
> Light-headed at the last? Our lives unreal
> Except as jeweled self-windings, a deathwatch
> Of heartless rhetoric I punctuate,
> Spitting the damson pit onto the plate?
>
> And if (weeks later, Athens) life still weighs
> Too heavily, why, leave the bulk behind.
> Give M. the bed.

The dark pun *deathwatch* and the testamentary feeling of leaving this or that possession to a friend or ex-lover have an ominous tone that goes beyond a farewell to Greece, or rather that brings into the foreground what such a farewell suggests—the end of youth, pleasure, one stage of life, and maybe life itself. "Santorini" ends with its tourists tired after a day's tramping: "We made on sore feet, and by then *were* made, / For a black beach, a tavern in the shade." Santorini does have a black volcanic beach, and a shady tavern is of course a welcome refuge from the blazing sun. Still, the poem seems to me to end at an entrance to the underworld.

A more cheerful view of time than "deathwatch," but still a valedictory one, characterizes our final passage. "Verse for Urania" is addressed at once to Merrill's Greek-American goddaughter on the occasion of her baptism and to the Muse. Above the crib of the sleeping baby a modern mobile revolves, and the mobile is reflected in the glass protecting a framed appliqué embroidered with the Greek legend "And this too will pass":

> Time drawing near, a clock that loses it
> Tells me you must wake now, pagan still.
> Slowly the day-glo minnow mobile twirls
> Above you. Fin-glints ripple in the glass

> Protecting an embroidery—your great-
> Grandmother's? No one remembers. Appliquéd
> On black: cross-section of a pomegranate,
> Stem and all. The dull gold velvet rind
> Full as a womb with flowers. Their faded silks entwine
> The motto KI ΑΥΤΟ ΘΑ ΠΕΡΑΣΗ—This too will pass.

And so it did pass on; Merrill willed this work of art to me. I lent the embroidery to the Hellenic Foundation's exhibit, but now it once again hangs in the foyer of the apartment where I live in New York. But he had already passed the image on by turning it into poetry: "for me," as Cavafy wrote, "the whole of you has been transformed into feeling." And the poetry was and is available to everyone who reads it, a possession for whoever wants to cherish it.

That the motto is Greek, and is both quoted in the original Greek and translated in Merrill's poem, brings us, in a way, back to the original spell cast by the Greek language. Who if not a sleeping baby is "simplified into a dream-figure"? The many long-standing ties between the poet and Greece proliferate (Merrill sponsored Urania's father's coming to America) even as they are inevitably dulled or distanced by the passage of time. This work of folk art, which memorializes Merrill's Greek connection, is itself captured and rescued from time by the poem. As the temporary custodian of the embroidery, I'll have to decide who to pass it on to. We are all owners of the poetry.

Part III

Poets and Poetics

Fructifying a Cycle

Homage to Alan Ansen

Autobiographical, solipsistic, mapped like a public park, laby-
rinthine as a dream—Alan Ansen's life and work, when I
happened into them in the fall of 1969, were oxymoronic.
They were also magnetic. The tall old house (since demol-
ished) on Alopekis Street in Kolonaki; the walls covered with
Corso collages; the looming bookshelves and drooping glad-
ioli, lilies, freesias, bought weekly from the Friday market and
watered daily—it's insufficient, of course, to describe Alan in
terms of his surroundings, but these details do convey some-
thing of the cluttered order, or cosmic chaos, of his place/
routine/self. My Greek already included *kalimera, kalispera,
kalinikta*—and was it James Merrill or Alan's friend Stavros
who used to wish Alan *kali routina?*

This routine proved more flexible than might at first ap-
pear. It was elastic enough, for example, to accommodate me.
Alan's house and life were immediately hospitable—and still
are; he is the most faithful friend imaginable. If the work took
longer to open itself to me, that was because I wasn't ready for
its distinctively lush flavor, its sometimes Gorgonzola-like
aroma.

Once acquired, the taste proved addictive. Nearly twenty
years after the first flush of my friendship with Alan, his
poetry—alert, patient, ineluctably itself—yielded itself up to
me. Its exhilarating mixture of order and chaos might have
been predicted from my first glimpse of Alan's menage, but

Afterword to *Contact Highs: Selected Poems of Alan Ansen 1957–1987*
(Elmwood Park, Ill: Dalkey Archive Press, 1989).

what now strikes me even more is the stillness and loneliness all the clutter doesn't quite conceal. If this is contradictory, the contradictions run so deep as to become a pattern. Reverence for the masters is balanced by the impulse to thumb one's nose at them; the splendid Ansenesque monomania ("I am the truth") is balanced (in the same line of poetry) by the admission that "the truth is a bore" ("Who"). A similar compression occurs in "An Occupational Hazard," where twinned oppositions bare their teeth at one another over the fence of a caesura: "Unmanageable poem, life of mine." The contrast is recapitulated in the title of Ansen's 1958 collection, *Disorderly Houses*.

"The joy of the horror and the horror of the joy," Ansen has summed up the subject of *Disorderly Houses*. "By instinct and biographical compulsion, I want the naked scream. By training and remembered satisfactions, I utter in patterns." In what follows I anatomize some of my favorite specimens of Ansen's patterned scream. This raucous yawp, which has been audible to a lucky few for thirty years now, is regularly redeemed from barbarity (however much Ansen yearns to be brutish) by reflectiveness, for many of Ansen's poems are majestically solipsistic broodings on their own occasion. To meditate on life and art, on influence and poetics, at the top of one's lungs, with supreme intelligence and self-consciousness—the paradoxes don't stop.

No wonder that my confused original impression was that this poetry was too discursive to be poetic—that each poem formed part of an enormous, dimly discerned argument. Given the intimacy of life and work ("unmanageable poem, life of mine") in Ansen's vision, the question of how to live is always turning into the question of how to work, and vice versa. Rather than supplying a monolithic or moralistic answer, the poems fashion multiple ways of posing or voicing the questions—ways that constitute a whole repertory of styles, from the meek to the exuberant, the hectoring to the satirical, often within the bounds of a single poem.

Consider the fable-like ditty "The Pitcher and the Well." Different typefaces indicate the two voices:

> *There was a little pitcher*
> *And they kept it very dry*
> *And they said if ever you get wet*
> *You'll be sure to die.*

The repressive Well (sounding, in its plural form, like the generalized *They* of Lear's limericks) is issuing a prohibition that might be rendered, "Don't live; it will kill you." Timidly, the Pitcher queries by way of reply:

> But aren't we made to get wet?
> More than that, to be full, maybe even overflow?

Progressively disobeying the increasingly angry Well, the Pitcher gets wetter and wetter, chipping, leaking, dying into life and art. Listen to its language by the end of the poem, as it interrupts the Well's final attempt at repression, "*Nasty little pitcher . . .*"

> Shut up, I'm working,
> Pouring a little, complicating and fructifying a cycle.
> The ululant leap in skivvies through snickering respectable
>   streets
> Or the spot of bother that suggests a rapid change of locale
> Are the price you pay for an anyway interesting exchange,
> Though the terms may vary with age:
> Pour pour gush gush pour
> Chip . . .

The defiantly clattering dactyls—sounding a bit like typewriter keys?—are a world away from the baby talk of the Pitcher's first response. (If one could hear Ansen read the poem, the voice would be dramatically different too; Ansen is one of the great poetic performers of his own and others' work.)

It's easy to enthrone the Pitcher as a tragic hero, courageously disobeying the injunctions issuing from the source of power, dying for the cause of art. But it would probably be more accurate to see in the Pitcher one version of the youthful self Ansen was to describe almost thirty years later, in his auto-biographical "Epistle to Chester Kallman" (*The Cell*, 1983) as "truculent, resentful, unrepressed, / At war with home, society and college"—a trio of forces not lightly to be dismissed (whatever the Pitcher's bravado and charm) in Ansen's work. These forces can be publicly pooh-poohed; they will be brooded upon in private.

For an endearing characteristic of Ansen's work is its fairness, its ability to see at least two sides to any important question. The zest with which Ansen mimes the voices and manners of variously dramatized attitudes ("The Pitcher and the Well" is only one of countless examples of such miming) shouldn't blind us to his essential impartiality; the dramatic brio highlights that impartiality by insuring that both sides be heard.

However variously keyed—from sarcasm to hysteria—the voices of the elders (home, society, college—the Well) are continuously noticeable in Ansen's poems, if not always as voices, then as mute reproaches.

> Was it for this that mother knit my socks,
> That father groaned on degrading commuter trains,
> Those brilliant papers, masterly examinations,
> Studies ripening for the fullness of time
> To perish on a relatively innocent bed?
>
> > ("The Public Hangman;
> > Or, In Praise of Capital Punishment")

> All the lousy clothes in a heap on the floor *that means work for somebody.*
>
> > ("The Double Take"; my italics)

Later, in "The Schedule" (*The Cell*), a celebration of domestic routine somewhat akin to Auden's *About the House*, work for somebody has become work for the poet himself, or "the domestic artist" as he now styles himself, calling the kitchen the

> Secret centre, decisive area,
> At once the jury box and judge's bench
> Where odorless good housekeeping, the stench
> Of bad and the uneasy mixture that

> Indifferent housework produces at
> No remove in time all come to judgment.
> The verdict is in on what the sludge meant . . .
>
>   ("The Hour of Housework")

Philosophically taking responsibility for cleaning up after himself, the poet is not so mellow with age that he avoids the stern terminology of jurisprudence when considering exactly that responsibility. Compare, at the close of the "Bicentennial Brood," also in *The Cell*, Ansen's metaphors for the generational struggle:

>   the civil suit brought against our parents
> In our youth . . . the criminal proceedings they
> Bring against us in our old age . . .

If, then, we cast a somewhat jaundiced eye at the "ululantly leaking" Pitcher as a Satanic/Miltonic/Byronic hero, we should probably be equally skeptical of the virtues of wetness as the Pitcher chips, pours, and gushes wholeheartedly. Romantic effusion is certainly in evidence here, but the spontaneous overflow of powerful feelings, however attractive at first glance, is an aesthetic that the very structure of Ansen's oeuvre, with its perpetual dialectic of yes and no, calls into question. Indeed, just such effusion may be the "occupational hazard" that gives a title to the poem excerpted here:

> Unmanageable poem, life of mine,
> How tempting to assert my control by the one
>   disastrous act of management,
> Whether it be on a hunt for putative maxima of intensity
> Or in an all too successful attempt to chasten
>   the happy wobblings of biological spontaneity
> To the iron insensitiveness of disciplined prosody.
>
> How really tempting is it?
> Not very.

The individualistic urge, it seems, is to assert control over the poem/life in one of the two opposing ways: either by seeking out a maximum of intensity (compare, from "Imperfect Tributes: A Shriek, a Song and a Discourse," this thumbnail sketch of Romanticism: "icy gentlemen who smoked hashish taking careful notes all the while") or else by deliberately subjugating spontaneity, bracing the "happy wobblings" of the organic sensibility with "the iron insensitiveness of disciplined prosody."

It hardly needs saying that Ansen has here sketched the Scylla and Charybdis of much more poetry than his own—a conflict treated with delightful wit in "A Fit of Something Against Something," his self-destructing sestina. If, to return to "An Occupational Hazard," neither alternative finally beckons, the reason is probably that both extremes are too simple.

The actual production of poetry, the work of writing itself, is often portrayed in relatively chastened, workaday terms, true to the physically describable aspects of the act:

> the scrap of paper and the cheap ballpoint.
> Sighing, shoulders stooped, I get up.
> Up and down, up and down.
> Hen tracks creep on the page.
>
> ("The Double Take")

> I acknowledge the presence of the outside world with five minutes of
> the latest news on the radio, then resume my seat or pace about, use
> my hand to write or scratch my head.
>
> ("The Hour of Creative Composition," *The Cell*)

As to what actually gets written, "the rest is silence here" ("Creative Composition"). It's easier to spell out what the poet must not do than what he does: "we must not / Forget our unconfounded persons in a rot / Of vague conformable good feelings" ("Imperfect Tributes").

A notable exception to the rule of not forgetting our persons, and a refreshing escape from awareness of the conflicting claims that elsewhere preoccupy him, is Ansen's "Heroin: An Ode." Essentially different from Ansen's other work ("my most visionary verse," he calls it in "Epistle to Chester Kallman"), the ode may be his closest approximation to the scribblings of the "icy gentlemen who smoked hashish while taking careful notes all the while," since it was written under the influence of heroin. Its provenance aside, the ode is a tranquil plateau above the crossfire of anxieties (how to live? how and what to write?) abounding in the poetry. A kind of doubleness persists ("The syndromes compete for an empty metabolism"); but the ode seems to limn a world where oppositions are canceled in an enchantment of suspended reality.

>Leftness and rightness
>Heaven overwhelms with a single pole,
>The axe of axes, at the verge of the absolute.
>
>Ask and insentience
>Holily calibrates the endless potentiation
>of
>The life where parallels meet.

Ansen's work might have developed very differently had he managed to remain in a world where "all spaces are alike," where "the whiteness is impermeable in either and all directions." Ansen has written that, when Auden read "Heroin," he "told me to take heroin again in order to make the poem clearer—something I don't think he would have advised everyone to do." Apparently, Ansen didn't follow the advice. He is essentially a poet of the cluttered and then cleaned-up interior, as the title of his first collection hints. His "fructifying cycle" is not the "unwhirled circle" of the ode but a more earthly process; his sacred space is numinous not with bright blankness but with books, art, and memorabilia (see, for one example, "The Cubicle" in *The Cell*). "Heroin" remains a beautiful anomaly in an oeuvre that is temperamentally social—argumentative, dramatic, satiric—with its monologue/routines, its dialogues, and its masques.

Because of the dramatic bent of Ansen's imagination, and also because of his honesty, the forces animating many of the conflicts in his work often take the shape of parents. The true source of inspiration is not heroin but one's human antecedents, both genetic and poetic. First, one's parents must be gotten out of the life and into the work: "Into our jemmying verses let us put our parents—after all, it's where they belong" ("Imperfect Tributes"). Once they are there, we can more clearly perceive the ancestors' indispensability and kinship:

> Now one no longer feels them as a threat
> To individuality, one pores
> Ever more frequently over the set
> One's life has taken from one's ancestors.
>
> The thrift, endurance and self-sacrifice
> Come to seem exemplary as one scans
> The ways in which one's father's ways suffice
> So unlike Hemingway's or Berryman's.
>
> ("Epistle to Chester Kallman")

> Where would we be without them, ancestors who raged
> As we do now against the fated limitations
> Imposed by what had been accomplished . . .
> . . . lavished many more
> Adjustments and discoveries on helpless heirs whose store,
> Embarrassment of riches, can't be utilized
> Till it is reacquired.
>
> ("Imperfect Tributes")

If the Pitcher's "Shut up, I'm working" captures the note of adolescence, a counterbalancing reverence and gratitude for the sources of the work are equally important in Ansen's poetry; the helpless heir can't make the most of his inheritance till he earns it again for himself. Ansen is positively worshipful of W. H. Auden and William Burroughs, the dedicatees of *Disorderly Houses* (presumably, though this may be too simple, Burroughs's is the disorder and Auden's the house) and remains modest about his status as "the keeper of the keeper of the flame" ("Epistle to Chester Kallman"). Lest the humility seem cloying, though, we should remember that Ansen's way of keeping the flame is to write. The self-deprecating gratitude in the following passages is, after all, in the context of a developing poetics of his own.

>   . . . our robbery bedecks
> More than our own apartments, happily reflects
> A smidgeon, a scintilla of lustre on the source
> Of our purloinings and convalidates the force
> For and to which we're grateful. At least we hope so
> As reconciled to our indebtedness we go
> To glorify our masters in fits of verbal violence
> Although the only perfect tribute would be silence.
>   ("Imperfect Tributes")

> The summer Allen spent with me in Venice
> Provided what I needed (bless him) to launch
> My overloaded rather sloppy pinnace
>
> On the sea of verse; and, as Leopardi says,
> Shipwreck is sweet to me in that sea. Perhaps
> We hope the act of composition unsays
> Unfitness for the journey without maps
>
> We're ultimately doomed to undertake.
>   ("Epistle to Chester Kallman")

In the last passage gratitude to another mentor, Ginsberg, is expressed in conjunction with a Pitcher-like willingness, even eagerness, to get wet. A line a bit earlier in the "Epistle" glances at Kafka's dictum that art is an axe to the frozen sea within us: "The frozen music had just begun to thaw."

Since Ansen is a poet of opposites, he might be expected to celebrate the impulse contrary to that of launching one's pinnace; and he doesn't disappoint us. To get drunk, sleep deep, curl up, hope it will all go away—Ansen treats these states of being as recurrent but in a sense unimportant aspects of life. No matter how morning-afterish the mood, the work of the day proceeds.

>   the ageing apprehensive infant
> Peeping forth at his dancing day . . . The moment of
>   confrontation passes, a neurotic order resumes:
> Journal, steak, prayers, transcriptions, lections
>   and a sour whiff of curses.
> The challenging sentry has allowed him to proceed.
>   ("In His Fortieth Year," *Believe and Tremble*)

        The shake awake,
Trembling, head throbbing, nauseously coughing, I scream
                    my eyes open.
Books scattered coffee-stained, ink spilled on the
                    rag rug,
The stinking dirty glass, the hateful gin bottle that
                    doesn't know when the party's over,
Brown stained underpants conspicuously unlike a flat
                    of truce,
All the lousy clothes in a heap on the floor that
                    means work for somebody
And the scrap of paper and the cheap ballpoint.
Sighing, shoulders stooped, I get up.
Up and down, up and down.
Hen tracks creep on the page.
Bitten nails weave the tenseness of suspended reality.
                                    ("The Double Take")

"The Schedule" is a more formalized version of what was early
a pattern: rededication each dawn to the work in hand. How-
ever neurotic, the order is also, clearly, a kind of salvation.

It is possible to take the hour-by-hour timetable elaborated
in "The Schedule" as a microcosm—from bed to bed / birth
to death—of human life. But a more programmatic mini-
history of humanity is "The Wheel," a poem that, moving
from birth to death in an individual's and perhaps a species'
existence, is eloquent on the loss involved with our gain of
consciousness.

            Chill breathings on the foetus as
    The puerperand creeps naked into outside, a
                    wide-spaced neighborhood, the neighbors
    God till our teeth sharpen and we circumvent our
                    family in search of other
    Conditions.

The more aware we become of the interdependence bred by
social complexity, the more we seem to lose: "Our gifted
speech the gift of our given / Dancing masters. . . ." Ap-
proaching the end of the cycle,

it is by no means without
A sigh of relief that we detect in our throats the
           compulsory death rattle, breathe in and then for the
           very last time breathe out.

Freighted with mortality, tinged by ironic awareness of our inescapable antecedents, often mordant—how dark is Ansen's work? Readers of this selection (and eventually, one hopes, of all the poems) will find their own answers. It's instructive to compare Ansen with his mentors, or with poetic peers. David Kalstone remarks in *Five Temperaments* that much of John Ashbery's work is undertaken in an atmosphere of "deliberate demolition," and the same might be said of Ansen's work. But—in strong contrast to Ashbery's pervasive plangency or Ginsberg's apocalyptic jeremiads—in Ansen we can constantly see the will to order reasserting itself. The trashed interior turns out to be an atelier of sorts. And Ansen's impulse toward order, however solidified it may seem in recent work like "The Schedule," keeps a certain jocundity (compare late Auden's depressive tone). For every sigh of resignation, such as we hear at the end of "The Wheel," a strain of hope is discernible somewhere in Ansen's work—an unsentimental, often ironically unlikely hope but nevertheless a gleam in the darkness.

I have personal reasons for feeling particularly moved by the beleaguered and fragile but real joys celebrated in a rare love poem, "Hortus Conclusus" (*Routines,* 1969–83):

> Peace
> Is a good we share
> To enjoy with a good conscience.
> The encounter of opposites
> In the playful stillness of embodied
> Charity is paradigmatic
> For a world continually under construction.
>
> When armed murderers from the
> State
> Or communities of ostentatiously
> Anarchic avant-garde sincere devil
> Worshippers are free to break in on

Whatever hidden inwardness we may
Try to build for ourselves behind a
Locked door, walls
Of varying thickness and an uninviting facade,
We must know the happy
Feeling of permanence a temporary grace to use as
Seems best to
More than ourselves, for we're
Creative creatures if you will.

The pattern of dark to light, of warring oppositions or threatening elements triumphantly transcended or resolved, is one of the figures in Ansen's carpet. A few examples must suffice. In "A Shriek, A Song and A Discourse" don't the first two elements of the title blend into, somehow give birth to, the relative modulation of the third? In "The Double Take" the dreamworld luxury (with a nod to "Invitation au Voyage") of the first stanza gives way to the squalid awakening of the second stanza, and the two worlds somehow merge their unreality and reality to make the real art of the final stanza:

Not in the sofas of expensive flesh and more expensive
    textiles,
Not in the flowers that sing to and grow in the senses,
But here, here alone, in the shiftless productive room
I am caught up in the life of the angels.

Most clearly, and in view of its position as opening poem in *Disorderly Houses,* most programmatically, "*The Newport News* has arrived in Venice for a week's stay" illustrates the pattern of up-down-up. Beautiful Venice in the present (st. 1) gives way to the past passions and lessons of "ugly Boston" (st. 2); and the two worlds come together in the final stanza:

Venice, I am not just part of your incomparable poem.
I have my own poetry and my own past.
God bless those American angels from the sea
For reminding me
"There is one story and one story only."
It promises all and performs nothing
Except to transform existence into life.

It's pleasantly typical of Ansen's work that this stanza both expresses gratitude to the unliterary "angels" of the Sixth Fleet and quotes from a revered poet—Robert Graves, whose "To Juan at the Winter Solstice" opens with the "There is one story" line.

In Ansen's vision this single story is often, and against the odds, a happy one. Its up-down-up curve traces what Northrop Frye has taught us to see as the mask of comedy—not necessarily the comedy of hilarity (though certainly Ansen can be one of the funniest poets I know of) but the comedy of resolution, restoration, and the fructifying cycle. The business of comedy, like that of any art, is deeply serious, as the last two lines of "*Newport News*" remind us: it "promises all and performs nothing / Except to transform existence into life."

This unflagging belief in the transforming powers of art has presided over Alan Ansen's remarkably honest and sustained exploration of the poetics of life and the life of poetry. Long may that exploration continue to flourish! "The rest is silence here," concludes "The Hour of Creative Composition," "but my hopes are for enduring resonance abroad and in the sky." Amen to those hopes; and, to Ansen's new readers, welcome to the work of a marvelous poet.

The Bowl Glows Gold

An Appreciation of Mona Van Duyn

Let's start in the kitchen.

Mr. and Mrs. Jack Sprat in the Kitchen

"About half a box,"
I say, and the male
weighs his pasta sticks
on our postal scale.

To support my sauce
of a guesswork rhymer
he boils by the laws
of electric timer.

Our joint creation,
my searchings, revisions
tossed with his ration
of compulsive precisions,

so mimics life
we believe it mandated
that God had a wife
who collaborated.

And cracked, scraped, old,
still the bowl glows gold.

(*Firefall*)

From *Discovery and Reminiscence: Essays on the Poetry of Mona Van Duyn*, edited by Michael Burns (Fayetteville: University of Arkansas Press, 1998).

At issue are the shared but contrasting joint preparation of a meal, the different ways men and women go about doing things, affection, time, Adam and Eve—a hundred pages' worth of experience and wry wisdom boiled down into laconic quatrains and topped off with a title that glances at a nursery rhyme. Very big and very small, domestic and cosmic—welcome to the world of Mona Van Duyn.

This world may seem cozy, but you need to keep your eyes open. The rich images in which Van Duyn's work abounds may be (to use the title phrase of her 1973 collection) merciful disguises. Flowers, birds, landscapes, food—how pleasurable, how immediately recognizable! But they're sneaky. If you read these poems with what Blake called single vision, then you are in danger of failing what Van Duyn, in a poem of that title, calls the Vision Test. Yes, the test in question is a real test that the poet must take when her "license is lapsing." But it is also more, or other, than that. For example, are we speaking of a driver's license here? And who is being tested? The applicant who must "master a lighted box of far or near" or the lady who administers the test, the "kindly priestess" with "her large, / round face, her vanilla pudding, baked-apple-and-spice / face in continual smiles"—a figure who before the end of the poem has been transformed into a "hen drinking clotted milk"? This test-giver (she has found the profession "poet" to be hilarious) is loath, as the actual test begins at the close of the poem, to administer it, for there is no telling how a poet will interpret the world:

> Her pencil trembles,
> then with an almost comically obvious show
> of reluctance she lets me look in her box of symbols
> for normal people who know where they want to go.

Earlier in "The Vision Test" (*If It Be Not I*) the speaker has imagined the others being tested as children who "come to grips with the rocks / and scissors of the world" at the maternal hands of the test-giver. But I am also rather tempted to envision these "normal people who know where they want to go" as male. In Van Duyn's 1993 Library of Congress lecture,

"Matters of Poetry," she tells us that certain male critics have been deceived by the domestic disguises in which her imagery is so rich into believing that her poems are only about the sources of their metaphors. As indeed they are—birds and bees, flowers and food, pantries and cabins. But they are also always about more.

> Ever since high school I have enjoyed writing extended meta-phor poems, writing about one thing in terms of another, which gives me a chance to play with the double meanings of words which can work simultaneously on both sides of the metaphor. . . . Blinded by the assumption that women do not have thoughts, do not write about ideas, reviewers who are incredibly talented at understanding the most difficult and pri-vate poetry by members of their own sex announce blithely that a poem of mine about the need for form in life and art is about walking a dog, or an analysis of friendship is about shop-ping for groceries.

Critics who cannot see Van Duyn's doublenesses surely fail her Vision Test.

Van Duyn's wise, funny, piquant poems are distinctive, but they are not freakish or unique. Should we place her in a tradition of female domestic poetry? In "Matters of Poetry" she writes rather impatiently, "Of course I write poems about everyday life—home, family, loved ones—every poet does, male or female."

Reading through Van Duyn's oeuvre recently, I kept being reminded of another writer. Who was it? I soon realized that Van Duyn's robust and witty sensuousness and her agile use of imagery "which can work simultaneously on both sides of the metaphor" recall Aristophanes, the sublime comic poet of fifth-century Athens. Like Van Duyn, Aristophanes, allergic to resounding abstractions and possessed of an allegorical bent, would pass the Vision Test with flying colors. Like Van Duyn, he can seem to be poking around the larder when his real subject is how to write a play or how to stop a war. For, again like Van Duyn, Aristophanes isn't shy about tackling such un-domestic topics as poetry or peace.

Looking through Aristophanes in search of a few specific instances of this unexpected but enchanting poetic kinship, I had the pleasant experience of refreshing my acquaintance with one of the funniest and slipperiest of great writers. Three examples, culled from only two plays, will have to suffice to illustrate my sense of the parallels between these two poets. (The translation by the ingenious nineteenth-century British cleric Benjamin Bickley Rogers has a jolly Gilbert and Sullivan flavor; Aristophanes' Greek uses far fewer words, giving the sense of a sketchier style and a more colloquial, fluent pace.)

In Aristophanes' *The Frogs,* Euripides, competing with Aeschylus in a contest as to who is the superior tragedian, claims that he has dieted down the tragic art from the bloated condition in which Aeschylus left it:

> When first I took the art from you, bloated and swoln, poor
>   thing,
> With turgid gasconading words and heavy dieting,
> First I reduced and toned her down, and made her slim and
>   neat
> With wordlets and with exercise and poultices of beet,
> And next a dose of chatterjuice distilled from books I gave
>   her . . .
>
> (939–43)

Of course, the comparison of tragedy—its theory and practice—to a patient in need of a healthful regimen is a cartoonlike allegory. But the cameo is so vivid that for a moment we forget about aesthetics and concentrate on the poor bloated girl of this before-and-after picture. Homeric similes work that way too, and so, often, do Van Duyn's poems; the scene or situation that is brought into being merely to vivify a comparison swiftly takes on an intense if miniature life of its own, as in these lines from "In the Hospital for Tests" (*If It Be Not I*):

> In twenty-four hours, the hefty nurse, all smiles,
> carries out my urine on her hip like a jug of cider,
> a happy harvest scene.

A little later in *The Frogs,* when Euripides boasts that his tragedies have taught the Athenians to be more canny in their household arrangements, Dionysius enthusiastically agrees with him in a passage that a single-visioned reader might easily mistake for a mere domestic riff. Note how Euripides' use of the single word *households* gives rise to a thumbnail sketch of groceries, china cupboard, and so on, which is both itself and something more:

> *Eur.* I taught them all these knowing ways
> By chopping logic in my plays,
> And making all my speakers try
> To reason out the How and Why.
> So now the people trace the springs,
> The sources and the roots of things,
> And manage all their households too
> Far better than they used to do,
> Scanning and searching What's amiss?
> And, Why was that? And, How is this?
>
> *Dio.* Ay, truly, never now a man
> Comes home, but he begins to scan;
> And to his household loudly cries,
> Why, where's my pitcher? What's the matter?
> 'Tis dead and gone my last year's platter.
> Who gnawed these olives? Bless the sprat,
> Who nibbled off the head of that?
> And where's the garlic vanished, pray,
> I purchased only yesterday?
>
> (975–88)

Those olives and garlic, that nibbled fish, would be right at home in a Van Duyn poem. They are so vividly themselves that I feel I've spied a fifth-century shopping list, and yet the point being made goes beyond crockery and sprats.

The punlike wit of doubleness is one of the many pleasures of reading Van Duyn; as she has told us in the lecture, it has also been one of her pleasures as a writer since the beginning of her career. A relatively lighthearted example, too long to quote in full, is "Emergency Room," subtitled "Turnpike, Anywhere, U.S.A." (*Firefall*).

Left on a table to die, a sandwich
can hardly believe this has happened to him.
Having heard it said so often about
his friends and neighbors, he still never expected
his own epitaph to be:
"They opened him up, took one look,
And just closed him up again."

In an adjoining section sufferers can see
disjointed bits of medical training taking place.
A long, nearly unmoving queue of them
suggests that primarily women, these days,
wish to be surgeons.
Each comes out, after what must have been
a long, laborious scrub,
looking annoyed, holding her dripping hands
well away from body and shoulderbag,
shaking them violently to dry in the air,
since the snappers-on of the rubber gloves
must be practicing someplace else.

Double vision again: the sandwich casts light on the patient,
the women on the surgeon, and vice versa. Vivid, rueful, mi-
nutely observed—it is funny but also not merely funny.

A third and final example from Aristophanes that savors
of Van Duyn is the passage in Lysistrata where the heroine
uses the example of spinning and weaving (quintessentially
women's work) to get a sense of political process, as it might
ideally be practiced by the war-weary women of Greece,
through a male official's thick head:

Ly.   Just as a woman, with nimble dexterity, thus with her
          hands disentangles a skein,
       Hither and thither her spindles unravel it, drawing it
          out, and pulling it plain.
       So would this weary Hellenic entanglement soon be
          resolved by our womanly care,
       So would our embassies neatly unravel it, drawing it
          here and pulling it there.
Mag.   Wonderful, marvelous feats, not a doubt of it, you
          with your skeins and your spindles can show;

> Fools! do you really expect to unravel a terrible war
> like a bundle of tow?

$$(567–72)$$

The magistrate has no patience either for Lysistrata's trope or for the laborious process she outlines for him—both sound too much like work, whether mental or manual. In the words of Van Duyn's poem, "Three Valentines to the Wide World," "Its view is simultaneous / discovery and reminiscence." *It* here is the poem, whose double gesture (reaching into the past for knowledge that can be applied to the future; reaching into memory for something to compare with something else) is exactly what Lysistrata is executing in a way so offensive to the magistrate.

I have not even touched on many aspects of Van Duyn's work, such as the range of her imagery; her skill as a writer of elegiac, celebratory, or other occasional poetry; her learning; her humor; her heartbroken zest for the things of this world; her recreation and preservation of her grandmother's bedtime stories. I've wanted to limit myself to such small matters as food, laughter, and tears; and even here my thoughts encompass much less than these subjects demand.

Food, then—two of the three examples cited from Aristophanes touch upon nutrition: poor, overweight tragedy (until Euripides got to her) and the Athenian householder's olives, fish, and garlic. If food, in its earthiness, is an essential ingredient of the comic vision, it isn't, in Van Duyn's work, ever only comic or comforting or familiar. (Van Duyn's beloved friend James Merrill knew that the answer is always YES and NO.) We've already seen that the wholesome face ("baked-apple-and-spice, vanilla pudding") in "The Vision Test" masks something at best bleak, at worst actively hostile. And blandly appetizing nursery food plays an unforgettable role in two poems that deal with the world of such food—the relation of daughter to mother, childhood to old age. In "The Stream" (*If It Be Not I*) the daughter takes her mother out to lunch, though "out" is inside the nursing home. The narrative fluency and ease of the following passage (reluctantly lifted from a poem too long to quote in full), its accommodation of details like cake and milk, move the reader toward the inevitable end as unconsciously, almost reassuringly, as every daily bite takes every one of us closer to our last supper.

> But they came with the lunch and card table and chairs
> and bustled and soothed you and you forgot the fears
>
> and began to eat. The white tablecloth, the separate
> plate for salad, the silvery little coffee pot,
>
> the covers for dishes must have made you feel
> you were in a restaurant again after all
>
> those shut-in years. (Dad would never spend the money,
> but long ago you loved to eat out with me.)
>
> You cleaned your soup bowl and dishes, one by one,
> and kept saying, "This is fun! This is *fun!*"
>
> The cake fell from your trembly fork, so I fed
> it to you. "Do you want mine too?" "Yes," you said,
>
> "and I'll drink your milk if you don't want it," (You'd
> lost twelve pounds already by refusing your food.)
>
> I wheeled you back. "Well, I never did *that* before!
> Thank you, Jane." "We'll do it again." "Way down *there*,"
>
> you marveled. You thanked me twice more. My eyes were
>   wet.
> "You're welcome, Mother. You'll have a good nap now, I bet."

Twenty-four lines later word comes that the mother has died, and the poem shifts, as it were, underground, to a meditation about the subterranean nature of love—a meditation that would not be anything like as moving without the lunch that precedes it. To read Van Duyn is less to marvel at how much she gets into her poems, so natural do they seem, than to be reminded of how very much of life most poets leave out.

"Delivery," the eloquent concluding poem of *Firefall* (1993), which takes place at the other end of life from "The Stream," features some of the same characters and even some of the same food. But the nourishing meal this time is a prelude not to death but to a kind of birth. If "The Stream" is sad, "Delivery" is uncanny. With utter lack of sentimentality, it notes the cruelty of adults, the confusion of childhood, the violence of revelation. In the first stanza the speaker remembers being five years old and weeping when not she herself but her friend Betty is scolded. This mix-up her mother finds funny and duly reports to the father in the second stanza:

> Soon it is supper time. In the kitchen they feed
> and talk, while I, invisible as I was
> in high-chair days, silently sit on Sears,
> wearing the weight of my big and bigger ears.
> "Well, you'll never guess what your crazy kid did today—
> if that wasn't the limit!" The story swells
> into ache in my stomach, then Dad's laughter and hers
> slice and tear like knives and forks and a worse
> hurt is opening in my middle; in familiar
> smells and muddle of voices, mashed potatoes,
> dimming light, hamburger, thick creamed corn,
> the milk-white chill, a self is being born.

> And is swept away through seething clots of minnow
> in the nearly hidden creek that weeps through the
>   meadow . . .

We are back in the subaqueous mysteries of subliminal feeling and uncontrollable change, the flow of emotions underlying the creamed corn and cold milk. Again, two worlds are here; this poem would be the poorer were either to be left out.

Finally, from the rich and varied bill of fare that could be gleaned from Van Duyn's poems, I choose not the ugly and seductive "Rascasse" (*Firefall*), the appetizing "Saleswomen in Baker Shops," or the stunningly observed and imagined "Goya's 'Two Old People Eating Soup' " but a passing reference to chowder. The narrative mastery of "The Stream" is in evidence here, too; the chowder isn't pressed into service as a trope, though of course it is a trope, but rather serves to introduce a heroic story of the birth of the child who gives the poem its title, "For Julia Li Qiu" (*Firefall*).

Ten days before we expected you, we gave
your mother and father fish and shrimp chowder
(in carp bowls, with Cloud Ears swimming in it darkly
—a bow to your heritage) lemon pie and tea.

Next morning, early, the telephone: "Surprise!
We're in the labor room. Water broke.
I think baby want chowder, want to come quickly,
but may take twenty-four hours. Talk now to Lili."

The birth turns out to be a terribly difficult one; "nothing
the childbirth classes taught them came true." While the
mother labors, the baby's poet father coaxes the infant along
by naming all the world's beauties, in gorgeous lines that,
according to the speaker, "friendship's telephone let me hear."
But these lines are clearly Van Duyn's lovingly embellished
version—her valentine, on Julia's behalf, to the world—of a
summons whose crux we have already encountered: "I think
baby want chowder, want to come quickly." The chowder and
pie and tea stand for the varied nourishment this world offers.
No wonder reading Van Duyn never fails to make me hungry.

Here are two quatrains of the incantation the speaker puts
into the father's mouth, translating his loving words in what-
ever tongue into the lingua franca of feeling but also into the
idiom of English verse:

"Come to the garden of life, its stony walkways
through rampant blossoms of glory and peace, its dappled
light and shade for the spirit's exquisite wooing.
There is nothing for you in death's dark fields of undoing.

"Come, come to love's tragi-comedy,
the masterpiece re-written for every body
and soul, its tears and laughter as near to each other
as Hell and Heaven are, as lover and brother."

At Sewanee a few years ago, when Wyatt Prunty did a superb
job of reading "The Vision Test" out loud, everyone in the
audience howled with laughter. And last week, sitting in the sun
rereading *The Frogs* and *Lysistrata* and confirming the affinities
between Aristophanes' unforgettable imagery and Van Duyn's

double vision, her "metaphors that make us meld" ("For Julia Li Qiu" again), I smiled with the joy of "simultaneous / discovery and reminiscence." "The Stream," on the other hand, and "For Julia Li Qiu" never fail—not on first reading nor second nor on umpteenth reading just this minute—to fill my eyes with tears. Haven't I just been reminded that "tears and laughter [are] as near to each other / as Hell and Heaven are, as lover and brother"? I am instructed and moved, admiring this easy-seeming mastery. Above all, I am grateful for the sense of renewal Van Duyn's marvelous poems give me.

The Ark of What Has Been

Elegiac Thoughts on Poetry

Recently faced with the task of renaming a course whose unappetizing moniker was "Technique of English Poetry," I was annoyed to find myself stumped: every new name that came to mind seemed politically incorrect. "Readings in the Lyric?" Too wispy. "Great Poems of the Western Tradition?" Too Eurocentric, elitist, exclusivist—I could already hear the cries. Until a happy coincidence led to my reading an article in *Harvard Magazine* about Helen Vendler's big poetry course, called something like "Poems and Poets," I didn't much like any of the new names I was able to come up with.

I like the prevailing sense of constraint still less. The strictures that box me in by condemning in advance not just the title of a course but all the assumptions behind that course's contents—what are they, exactly? The mandate isn't precisely for what used to be called relevance. If there's a keyword now, it might be *inclusiveness:* the push for representation of all that has gone unrepresented, for centering what has been marginal, for foregrounding (or privileging or valorizing) what has been—underprivileged? Teachers of literature are being asked to wield a syllabus as an instrument, a weapon, of social justice.

Rooting out entrenched, privileged ways of thinking is uncomfortable work at best. But beyond the effort to adjust and learn is a sense of strain it's time to acknowledge. The half-hidden sense of coercion attendant on curricular changes is an

From *Associated Writing Programs Chronicle* 23, no. 6 (May 1991).

insidious source not only of strain but of distortion. In bending to the winds of change, we may not manage to become paragons of social justice and fairness to all; but we can very easily cease to be ourselves. Striving to be scrupulously fair to every conceivable group, to marginalize no one, a teacher of literature inevitably finds herself giving short shrift to everyone. Is this an improvement? Permit me to doubt it. Permit me to question whether it is desirable to stretch a syllabus until it resembles the pleated jaws of a python preparing to swallow a cow— especially when what enters even so capacious a maw must be predigested, broken down into labeled component parts.

For our conscientious expansion of the canon goes hand in hand with a relentless process of segmentation. Just to enlarge the tradition is too simple; there must be quotas, and so the newcomers wear their ethnic costumes, and poetry is shattered into poetries: Chicano, Chicana, gay, lesbian, Native American, and so forth. Ten years ago the disappearance of the image of the melting pot was touted as a change in popular consciousness. Now we have something ranker, yeastier; sour mash? rising dough? Adrienne Rich praises Joy Harjo as "one of the real poets [as versus the fake poets?] of our mixed, fermenting, end-of-the-century North American imagination." Wesleyan's new catalogue describes Harjo as "a powerful voice for her Creek (Muscogee) tribe ('a stolen people in a stolen land'), for other oppressed people, and for herself."

The trouble with such praise is that literature, if it works at all, has to work—has always worked—in concentric rings. Poetry or fiction that fails to make the leap from self to world is sooner or later swallowed up in the gaping maw not of the syllabus but of oblivion.

What seems to be happening is that the ethnic identity or political stance of a writer is perceived as more crucial for his or her work's success than that work's quality. The pressure can be conceived of as spatial: even an expanded canon can hold only so many works, so we are forced to bump some. But it's also temporal: the new works we take on board have not yet stood the test of time, yet they are catapulted from private to public, from notebook to textbook, with no interval in which to ripen.

Some of the pressure touches me even more closely. In the self-righteous and humorless air of English departments these days, what one inhales is more than a mandate to rename a course, expand a syllabus—tasks that after all need doing. Attendant on this mandate is another one: that I mask and muffle my own literacy, my classical training, my cultural background—in other words, that I disown the tradition to which I happen to belong and which has nurtured me. This demand makes itself felt not so much through the bureaucratic channels of the university as in the pages of some poetry journals.

A recent issue of *American Poetry Review* (19, no. 1 [Jan.– Feb. 1990]) contains a long essay in which Ira Sadoff attacks the "dangerous nostalgia" of that obnoxious crew the New Formalists—a loosely defined group of largely American poets between thirty and fifty years old who have failed to condemn meter (especially iambic pentameter) in particular and poetic form in general as obsolete. Sadoff's diatribe echoes many recent essays and reviews which perceive poetry as ancillary to more or less desirable political postures. Indeed, Sadoff's piece represents a salient trend in the criticism of formal verse. Like Wayne Dodd's remark that the New Formalists merely espouse "the Reaganism of poetics—Reaganetics," or like Diane Wakoski's assertion that "there is a new conservatism in this country, and it is in our poetry exactly as in our politics," Sadoff's way of proceeding is to line up certain—to him—objectionable poetic predilections with the kind of conservative political positions he finds equally reprehensible.

Such conservative positions, in Sadoff's view, are espoused with apparent unconsciousness by the benighted perpetrators of formal verse. They (a favorite critical term of Sadoff) can't see the political significance of their poetic practice, or of their taste; but don't worry, the perspicacious critic won't miss the point. Sadoff writes:

> We live in a world of many cultures, many voices; our poetries are enriched by otherness, by many different kinds of music and varieties of meters. Their narrow-minded appreciation of cadence and music unconsciously create [*sic*] a kind of cultural imperialism.

The fallacies in this brief passage take a little teasing out. Notice, first, the segmentation of all writers and apparently readers as well (since what is at issue is "appreciation" as well as writing) into "us" and "them." By writing in, or even by enjoying, certain features of poetry that are loosely but disapprovingly tagged "cadence and music," "they" are irrevocably, if also inadvertently, taking sides.

One's enjoyment of certain styles of art (which is the idea Sadoff's phrase "narrow-minded appreciation" crudely expresses) does of course represent a choice, perhaps even a decided preference of one mode over another. Such a preference may possibly imply a conscious rejection of alternative choices; just as possibly, it implies no such rejection. Our minds are wonderfully elastic where literature is concerned, which is why, within limits, expanding the canon is a good idea. For those who love books, increase of appetite can often grow by what it feeds on. It is a common experience that enjoying one kind of style often opens out one's appreciation for other styles. But, while I cherish the opportunity to read widely, I also defend my right to prefer some poems to others. Sadoff contrasts the prejudice of a writer/reader who appreciates only cadence and music with an open-mindedness that as soon as one thinks about it proves to be mythical. When he describes "our" multi-voiced culture only to slam it in the face of a narrow-minded "them," Sadoff is being unfair to both sides.

Although a reader's or writer's preference for a certain artistic style may reflect (or resist) prevailing cultural norms, such a preference does not in itself constitute cultural imperialism. Imperialism requires conscious action, some of which we have recently had a chance to contemplate in the cases of the Mapplethorpe and Serrano exhibits. The cutting off of funds from artists whose work is unacceptable to prevailing ideology is closer to cultural imperialism than is a private propensity to prefer blank verse to free verse. In any case, Sadoff has his imperial metaphor backwards. It isn't they (the New Formalists, red-faced colonials in solar topees and puttees) who wish to push imperiously aside certain ways of thinking about or reading, let alone writing, poetry—to proclaim them artistically retrograde because they are politically repugnant. It is Sadoff ("we") who itches to do exactly this. The charge of cultural imperialism as Sadoff wields it turns out to be a boomerang.

No poet I know would want to deny the variousness of the world. But the state of any particular poem is the state of any particular human being: contingent, individual, caught in time. We may read all the world's literature, but we still, even in the spurious breathlessness of Postmodernism's vortex, write more or less alone, a poem at a time. Sadoff, who talks of many cultures and many voices but strongly disapproves of at least one particular poetic voice, seems to subscribe to the late Raymond William's ideal of a common culture, an ideal described by John Bayley as "not only deadening in itself but depressingly utopian, assuming as it does that the human heart should not only feel but think and believe the same things" (*Times Literary Supplement,* Feb. 23–Mar. 1, 1990, 188).

Bayley links literature and politics in a way that allows much more diversity than does Sadoff's lip service to a polyphonic culture. He writes: "If all literature must be political it must also be personal, geographical, private, two-faced, idiosyncratic, perverse, full of unresponsible joy, intimacy, despair." Intimacy, the human scale, is crucial. We do not hold our poems up for approval to the Committee of Public Safety or the UN Charter. Poets are private human beings writing for other human beings in an inevitably local idiom. Carried to their logical extreme, wouldn't the multi-voiced cultures lauded by Sadoff blend into a global homogeneity? I have in mind some sort of technological advance that would permit the politically correct poet to write in every conceivable fashion simultaneously. This would be the only way to avoid such undesirable slips from perfect equality as privileging one style, subject, or even language over another.

The back cover of the same issue of *APR* that contains Sadoff's essay features a poem entitled "Absence of Poetry" by the Brazilian Adelia Prado. The flat-footed banality of the lines as translated by Ellen Watson may mean no more than that Prado's particular voice fails to come across in English. Yet one burden of this poem is apparently a desire for art, a

yearning for transcendence despite the cultural blankness re-
ferred to in the title.

> He who made me took me away from plenty;
> forty days he's been tormenting me in the desert.
> The politician died, poor guy.
> He wanted to become president and didn't.
> My father wanted to eat.
> My mother wanted to wander.
> I'm in favor of the revolution but first I want a rhythm . . .
>
> I, who said in the town square (exposing myself)
> "Let's dance, you ragamuffins, follow the beat,
> the Kingdom is implicit but real"— . . .
>
> I see the mango tree against the black cloud,
> my heart warms,
> once more I delude myself I will make the poem.

Although I don't know what Prado's politics are, it seems
hard to reconcile this wistful desire for artistry in a bleak and
hungry world with the expectations of a critic like Sadoff, for
whom the "unconscious cultural imperialism" of formalist
poets goes hand in hand with political as well as aesthetic
conservatism:

> One only has to look at the tonalities of poems from other
> historical moments, however, to understand the neoformalists'
> resignation . . . their desire . . . to resist change and the possibil-
> ity of change formally, intellectually, emotionally.

Sadoff never tells us which "other historical moments" he
has in mind. Poets like Prado or—in the same issue of *APR*—
the Argentine Olga Orozco inhabit our historical moment but
have little to do with the traditions of Anglophone poetry.
Certainly, neither can be accused of formalism old or new, and
both come from countries where a "declining political culture"
has given rise to recent and repeated revolutions. Yet Prado's
poem is full of longing for beauty, and Orozco's far more
accomplished work is unquestionably elegiac. Not that Orozco
is lamenting the loss of a repressive political order; elegy as

temperament, as genre, can cut through a historical moment or run counter to it.

In "Far Away, From My Hill," translated by Mary Crow, Orozco's topic is a quintessentially lyric one: the losses and beauties of our passage through time.

> Perhaps you have lived only what,
> burning, leaves no more than dust of immortal sadness,
> what greets you, through memory,
> an eternal dwelling that, receiving us, bids us goodbye.
>
> You don't ask anything, ever,
> because there's no one now to answer you.
>
> But there, over the hills,
> your sister, memory, with a young branch still between her
>   hands,
> tells once more the unfinished legend of a foggy country.

Peter Sacks notes in his masterful 1985 study *The English Elegy: Studies in the Genre from Spenser to Yeats* that our age is replete with elegies and elegy-like poems, a fact that in itself calls for neither praise nor blame. The critic's task is to discriminate, not to prescribe. Sadoff, however, set off by the faintest whiff of elegy, complains that "at least two dozen poems" in Robert Richman's 1988 anthology *The Direction of Poetry* "evoke the *a priori* condition of loss and diminishment," as if no poetic good could ever come of such an opening gambit.

Whether Sadoff is primarily faulting a literary tradition, a personal temperament (or cluster of temperaments), or a political stance, his indignation is preposterously naive. Is not our human situation indeed in many ways one of loss and diminishment, and has not much great literature from all historical moments—from Homer and the Bible onward—acknowledged this fact? Philip Larkin said (tongue in cheek as always but not without truth) that deprivation was to him what daffodils were to Wordsworth. One can point to Larkin's conservative political stance; but what of the politics of another celebrant of deprivation, diminishment, and loss, Samuel Beckett? Mourning voices, some of them quite young voices, can be heard in this country too. Christopher Merrill, a New Mexico poet, observes that "contemporary poets who write about nature do so for a readership on the verge of being 'after-comers' to the beauty of the whole planet." Hope for the future is fine, but what if in the meantime elegy is being forced upon us? Sadoff names no writers of whose "tonalities" he approves until late in his essay (we'll come to them soon); but his blanket dismissal of work he accuses, on the grounds of its elegiac mode, of celebrating a moribund political order is reminiscent of Marxist critics who denounced Mann, Joyce, Proust, and even Kafka as fascists.

Exactly the same immunity to irony that makes Sadoff proof against the tonalities of such a poet as James Merrill enables him (Sadoff) to write:

> Clearly the great poets of Latin America and Eastern Europe live inside history, and their imaginations are enlivened by that perspective. . . . American writers are too often only witnesses, tourists, to most human suffering and pleasure.

It's nice to know that certain fortunate poets—once again unnamed but indisputably "great"—have ringside seats not only to history but to pain, joy, love, and death. It simplifies our lives to be able to prune from our syllabi the works of such historical drones as Emily Dickinson or Cavafy, A. E. Housman or Elizabeth Bishop, none of whom had the luck to engage in public events. The men with AIDS with whom I run a weekly poetry workshop might be expected to know something about extremity and courage, but, no, I guess they're on the wrong barricades. To live, read, think, love, lose, remember, and write—every one of these acts is apparently too encapsulated in bourgeois privacy to qualify for Sadoff's greatness.

Sadoff's sentimental assumption seems to be that a life inside history is a kind of poets' paradise of empowerment, vision, and hope. I wonder. Some of the great poets of this century have faced up to the discouraging conditions of their, and our, time. "Poetry makes nothing happen," says Auden. And Brecht writes in "To Posterity":

I ate my food between massacres.
The shadow of murder lay upon my sleep.
And when I loved, I loved with indifference.

I looked upon nature with impatience.
So the time passed away
which on earth was given me. . . .

For we know only too well:
Even the hatred of squalor
Makes the brow grow stern.
Even anger against injustice
Makes the voice grow harsh. Alas, we
Who wished to lay the foundations of kindness
Could not ourselves be kind.

(Trans. H. R. Hays)

But Auden and Brecht go unmentioned in Sadoff's polemic.

One way we can live in history is through the imagination, through knowledge—in a word, through reading. Sadoff's hands-on poetic, which gives credit for life experience while subtracting points for bookishness ("American writers are only witnesses"), disregards two simple facts about how people function. First, as I've said earlier, each of us can write only one poem at a time; the art dooms (or privileges) us to be univocal, incomplete. But, second, there is almost no limit to the number of poems we can read, absorb, think about. Although most poems that have survived through the ages were probably not designed primarily as instruments of propaganda, nevertheless poems can and do teach. Sadoff, predictably, believes art should propagandize. Thus, he writes of Carolyn Forché's "The Colonel" that the poet "didn't see sufficiently into her experience to transform the consciousness of any reader who didn't already share her values." But such consciousness-raising need not be poetry's mission. Forché's flat, suspended tone in her poem is surely intentional; it seasons the raw meat of her theme with subtlety, which, along with elegy, proves to be a bête noire for our critic.

Late in Sadoff's piece it comes as a relief to discover two poems he actually approves of. But while I find both C. K.

Williams's "Still Life" and Gerald Stern's "Behaving like a Jew" quite likable, it's hard not to notice that, when it comes to work he enjoys, Sadoff relaxes his impossibly austere standards of historicity, relevance, political correctness, and scope in order to praise poems whose strength is distinctly personal.

Both these poems recall a private moment; furthermore, each is a kind of elegy—Williams's for a moment from his youth, Stern's both for a dead opossum and, by extension, for a temperament, a people, a way of being. To be sure, both poems are aware of their own procedures. Williams laboriously dismantles his nostalgic memory in long lines that are both rambling and meticulous, both vague and specific:

> I don't know then how much someday—today—I'll need it all,
> how much want to hold it,
> and, not knowing why, not knowing still how time can tempt
> us so emphatically and yet elude us,
> not have it, not the way I would, not the way I want to have
> that day, that light.

And if Williams thinks about himself thinking, Stern watches himself watching, sketches his own imminent choice of behavior:

> —I am going to be unappeased at the opossum's death.
> I am going to behave like a Jew
> and touch his face, and stare into his eyes,
> and pull him off the road.

Two decidedly self-conscious poems, then, that precisely by virtue of Williams's and Stern's reflexive gazes into their respective poetic mirrors seem to escape the charge of sentimental idealism leveled by Sadoff against Richman's anthology as a whole.

My problem with Sadoff's praise of these two poems is that any poem worth its salt is conscious of its own procedures. The poet's many choices at every level of language register his or her awareness of and innovations within a tradition. Poems that fail to function within this complex frame of reference, that try for immediacy by pretending (or even believing) that poetry was invented just this minute, strive for originality only to fall into the shallowness and banality that are the besetting sins of the poetry of every age, buttoned or unbuttoned, formal or free. Such banality is also too often the result if we stretch our aesthetic to encompass every conceivable voice, every crucial historical moment. If, in Mark Rudman's phrase, we always "leap directly to the universal," then the pungent ironies, the rich resonances, the inherited idiosyncrasies of much of the world's great lyric poetry are in danger of being pushed aside, flattened out, erased.

In the lyric less is more. Lyric poems have always been brief, not encyclopedic. Though it has become politically suspect to say so, they work by exclusion. Williams's "Still Life," set in a pastoral summer scene, marginalizes the adolescent romances of say, an inner-city youth; in "Behaving like a Jew" Stern gives short shrift to (let's say) the U.S. government's depredations of Native American lands. We take for granted, as we should, that in order to achieve their effects these poems, in obedience to generic laws, set up thematic boundaries that (in these cases) constitute their chief formal equipment and which, within the modest personal confines of their respective ranges, work well.

But these pleasant poems look not only self-caressing but positively flabby in their self-indulgence compared to three lyrics from *Late Settings,* the 1985 collection of one of the chief whipping boys of Sadoff's essay—James Merrill. Sadoff indignantly misreads the conclusion of "Clearing the Title," a long poem from the volume, but doesn't refer to such lapidary short pieces as "Casual Wear," "Popular Demand," or "Channel 13." It's a safe bet that the deft elegance of these pieces would in any case arouse Sadoff's ire. But, in addition, Merrill's control of image and tone is disconcertingly harnessed to a dark vision of a poisoned world, terrorism, species made extinct. We might expect a recognizable voice, well-earned idiosyncrasies, from a master poet in this, his twelfth collection; what we get is a willed and utterly authoritative impersonality, whose only concession to personal tone is often (in Stephen Yenser's words) "a coldly bitter" edge.

It is as if Merrill has renounced mere personality as one more doomed cultural artifact. These are poems of destruction and reduction, which observe human behavior and its results with enthralling steadiness. The ludicrousness of Sadoff's requirement that poets live "inside history" becomes obvious when we read these poems. Would they have been more convincing had Merrill actually been present at the terrorist bombing or in the fallout shelter? We should be grateful, not impatient, at the personal well-being of a poet who can do more than simply report from the front lines. The voice in these pieces does indeed wear a faintly reportorial guise, but Merrill is more vatic than journalistic. Prophecy does more than foretell; as Homer knew, the *mantis* can inform us of what has happened, what is happening, and what will happen. "Casual Wear" is set in the historical present; it could, as we say, happen any time. "Popular Demand" 's present and perfect tenses belie our desperate hope that this vignette of a world after "the bright, chromosome-garbling burst" will never happen ("It would seem the worst / Has happened, who knows how—"). And "Channel 13," dealing neither with a specific and random act of violence nor with an ultimate explosion but with an inexorable process, is written, as Yenser notes, "in a chilling past tense, as though nature had already vanished down the black hole at the center of the dying tube."

The cool indignation of these dark late poems never prevents Merrill's images from executing their elegant acrobatics. To be struck dumb by horror is only one response; most people, and certainly most poets, answer the writing on our collective wall with more words. That this is the way we human beings operate is a paradox that Merrill sets before us in poems that refuse to mitigate either the guilt or the ingenuity of our species. The two belong to the same world, just as the Adamic naming of animals at the beginning of "Channel 13" is of a piece with the image of the ark at the poem's close. Yenser writes:

> These poems are the more affecting for the steadfast eschewal
> of scapegoats and simplification. . . . "Channel 13," seeming to
> discover the origin of "our ultimate 'breakthrough' lenses" in

Adam's naming of the animals, implies that the extinguishing
of other species is inextricable from our pursuit of knowledge.

But if Merrill avoids scapegoating, he nevertheless has little
use for consolation. Although the animal-show hosts' voices in
"Channel 13" are "self-excusing," Merrill excuses, and holds
out hope for, no one. The brief arc of rising spirits in "Popular
Demand," like the question "World without End?" in "Radi-
ometer," is cut off with a peremptory (in one case a ferocious)
imperative. All our instincts, both personal and literary, yearn
for reassurance, for consolation that these barbed poems do
not provide.

Accusation and counter-accusation, New Formalist and free
verse—the pendulum keeps swinging. Any way of writing a
poem exacts a penalty. But, questions of rhyme and meter
aside, it is Sadoff's vision of poetry that is—if not precisely
nostalgic—sentimental at heart. For what he sees as the essen-
tial role of poetry—a social and political role—is tied to a
version of the Golden Age with which he optimistically pitches
forward into the future. The sentimental glow of the typical
New Formalist elegy excoriated by Sadoff emanates from the
past; for Sadoff it is the future whose rosy glow enables him to
ignore the paradoxes and ironies of the present.

To be sure, many contemporary elegies are flaccid, self-
regarding, mediocre; so is most poetry of any time. But to in-
dict the form itself or the mood behind it is just a way to
sidestep the legitimate pain of mourning. It is much easier to
label James Merrill a racist (based on the grotesque misread-
ing of a single image) than it is to imagine on a global scale and
write in a style honed both by technical expertise and personal
outrage. It is easier to blame a poet for writing in a certain
style than to understand what the poet is using that style to
say—particularly if the style is a highly developed, elaborate
one. It is easy to dismiss irony and complexity, but one pays
the price of missing the sharp edge beneath the silken surface.

Judging by the Williams and Stern examples, Sadoff ad-
mires poems that, like a freshman composition essay, tell us
exactly what they're doing. I think we need poems of greater
tension and complexity, which make demands on us but also

offer rewards. Merrill's late political poems undo me. They make me *feel* what I only dully knew, that in our time we are on the edge of an abyss—perhaps many abysses. There is terror in the knowledge, and rage; there is also, inextricably intertwined, what Hart Crane called "the silken skilled transmemberment of song."

That song must not be allowed to vanish in "the snug electronic ark of what has been." The most important part of my task as a teacher is to bear witness to, to explain, even to "aftercomers," what I understand best of the complex, and always timely, beauty of a heritage that is theirs—or will be, if they have a chance to be taught it.

Two Letters from New York

I

In "Matters of Poetry," her 1993 lecture at the Library of Congress, then Poet Laureate Mona Van Duyn spoke eloquently of the overstuffed condition of poetry criticism in the United States these days:

> who has not read the gorgeous, inflated rhetoric of praise in a review and then suddenly burst into laughter at the quoted passage the critic has been talking about, the bad, flat, inept lines that provoked that incandescent praise?

This kind of ludicrously incandescent praise is alive and well in a recent letter to *PMLA,* the official organ of the Modern Language Association, in which phrases like "elegiac ambiguity," "a wry sense of the anxiety of influence," and "melancholy resignation" are slathered over a poem typical lines of which include "O, I don't give a shit," "the guy was a loon," and "fucking dead."

The ways we think about literature necessarily involve ourselves, whether we are writers worrying about their audience or readers brooding about the writer behind the work. But the very notion of the self appears to be undergoing if not quite effacement, then progressive fragmentation into a cluster of entities. At a recent PEN symposium of lesbian and gay writers, a novelist said: "When I was asked, on a radio show, 'Do you think of yourself as a Lesbian writer?' I had to answer 'Let me have thirty seconds to think about it, because I haven't thought about it in a long time.'"

From *PN Review* (1993–94).

> I think of myself [she went on] as a writer and a lesbian, and as
> a writer and white, and as a writer and a woman, and as a writer
> and a southerner, and as a writer and an American, and as a
> writer and an alcoholic. All these identities have influenced
> how I see the world. Literature belongs to the dispossessed.

And as the self splinters into shards before our eyes, the
notion of audience seems to undergo a similar process of dis-
mantling, until the imagined readership of a given work of
literature comes to consist of just about the same number of
potential members as the component selves of the author that
audience is reading. "I think I'm writing for about six people,"
said the novelist quoted earlier. "One is my editor . . . Another
is a straight woman academic . . . Another is my mom."

One would like to think that from this process of crazing a
kind of shattered pointillist miracle emerges, transforming the
many dots into one sharp shape or even a unified luminous
blur—anything to convey the illusion of wholeness. If such a
metamorphosis does occur, it is certainly, now no less than at
any other time in the history of literature, the exception rather
than the rule.

A limited number of selves is all most of us can manage to
cobble together. Do we (consciously or not) divest ourselves of
most of them when we write, or do we rather concentrate on a
segment or two at a time—the white alcoholic, say, rather than
the working-class lesbian? That there is no simple answer to
this question may mean that the question itself is wrong, or at
least incomplete, since it fails to take account of our willing-
ness to put on new selves, to forget the old boundaries, when
we write.

To imagine a life, to translate a voice—such ventures, never
easy to pull off, are all the harder when one is pinned down
like Gulliver by the innumerable threads of race, gender, sex-
ual orientation, class, region, ethnicity, addiction of choice. . . .
And yet to break all these clinging threads, to transcend the
insistently proclaimed particulars of our time, is no guarantee
of artistic triumph either.

A recent book of poetry, Carolyn Forché's *The Angel of His-
tory,* spreads its wings grandly above all mere particulars—and

was received by critics as a mystical revelation. Part of the awe behind this exaggerated veneration was surely an honest response to the fact that Forché was writing for an audience of a lot more than her mother, a straight editor, and so on; that moreover Forché in writing this poem clearly had not felt constrained by the biographical details of her own life but could dare to inhabit other selves.

The writer who for the moment is neither taking a stand nor sitting down to write could do worse than stand up for a few minutes, among a group of others, to read the words of someone else—not one more refraction of the self but another person. Dante, for example. On the evening of Maundy Thursday, in the Cathedral of St. John the Divine, thirty-three poets read the *Inferno* aloud, in translations each had chosen, from nine or so till dawn. The attendant reverberations weren't merely acoustical, as Sinclair encountered Binion or Robert Pinsky talked back to Longfellow. Through all the renderings and in all our various voices Dante could be heard, here describing, there exhorting, always crisply narrating, pressing onward, never pausing to wonder which of his selves was lost.

I don't think any of the readers felt that he or she was addressing only a handful of people. The church was pretty full to start with, and more people drifted in and out as the night wore on. We were our shattered selves—father of sick child, orthodox woman up for tenure, visitor from Vermont, lady with broken leg, newly separated father, recently uncloseted poet—and so it went. Except that it didn't go that way at all. Speaking someone else's words, we shared in a journey larger than ourselves.

II

Let it be understood that any account of the New York literary events (chiefly poetry) I attended in the fall of 1993 represents only a fraction of goings-on about town. The pace of literary life in Manhattan is such that to get to the PEN Writers for Sarajevo benefit (David Rieff, Susan Sontag, Mary Gordon,

Tony Kushner, and a score or so of others) will probably mean you miss the bard from out of town whose visit was scheduled months earlier. If I fail to describe the Scandinavian Poetry Festival at Cooper Union or the Poet Laureates' group reading at the Cathedral of St. John the Divine, it's not because of any hidden agenda; I simply happened to miss those events.

Sir Stephen Spender once sagely noted that the Auden group never met as a group. Similarly, the essential fact to keep in mind about New York literary life is that there is really no such thing. This isn't to say that from reading to reception to party certain faces don't recur; it's simply to emphasize that no one event or even series epitomizes the literary season. It's possible, of course, to carve out aesthetic domains along geographical lines—we have so-called Uptown and Downtown music, so why not poetry? But any such lines of cleavage are as rigid and reductive as the tirelessly applied terms of formalism, neoformalism, expansionism, and so on—labels over which further stickers are now being plastered, this time denoting gender, class, race, ethnicity, and sexual orientation.

In her recent memoir, *Curriculum Vitae,* Muriel Spark quotes a Poetry Society official's comment on her depiction of the London poetry scene in the late 1940s: "Plus ça change! The poetry world seems inherently faction-ridden and fissiparous." Here, then, are twelve events I recall from the fissiparous, and already fast-fading, fall season. The most obscure sounding were not necessarily the least worth attending.

October 9. A group reading, at the East 96th Street branch of the New York Public Library, of poets published over the years in *Pivot,* a little magazine based in New York and edited by Martin Mitchell. Most of the audience of fifty or so seem to be poets, some of whom have come from as far afield as Washington, D.C. Good manners are maintained; no one exceeds the two-poem per person limit, and many poets read only one poem. I shepherd two out-of-town poets back to Martin's for the reception, and we discuss both the often fatal fascination of the Civil War as a poetic subject (news to many on the downtown circuit, no doubt) and the phenomenon of the numerous poetry publications that impose criteria not only of technique but of subject matter on all would-be contributors (write a triolet about the spring).

October 17. The annual candlelight Vespers service, at the immense, unfinished Cathedral of St. John the Divine, at which two deceased American writers are inducted into the Cathedral's Poets' Corner. As usual in this version of Poets' Corner, one of the writers is primarily a poet and one is not; this year the two to be honored are Henry Wadsworth Longfellow and Stephen Crane. (Twain and Poe, Emerson and Stevens, Faulkner and Eliot, Frost and James, Moore and Wharton, Robinson and Thoreau and Melville are all ensconced already, and I've surely forgotten someone.) My favorite feature of this ceremony is the fact that four (living) American writers read brief excerpts from the work of their predecessors and that they do so without the fulsome introductions that are a tedious feature of readings in New York. This evening Dana Gioia and Richard Wilbur say a few words about Longfellow— well, Gioia says more than a few—and Crane falls to Daniel Hoffman and Alfred Kazin. The conclusion of "The Open Boat" as read by Kazin tosses the hermeneutic ball tantalizingly to the attentive audience, since the story ends "and they felt that they could then be interpreters."

October 24. An eight-hour marathon of readings interspersed with musical interludes—the whole grandly entitled "The Republic of Verse"—is held at the 92d Street Y to mark the publication of the two-volume anthology of nineteenth-century American poetry magisterially edited for the Library of America by John Hollander. Twenty or more writers (all American, not all poets), chosen on the basis of our ability to do "elocutionary justice" to the poems, read chronologically arranged excerpts from the anthology. Successive segments take us from Joel Barlow, FitzGreene Halleck, and Thomas Cole through Whitman, Dickinson, Longfellow, and on toward 1900—but I didn't stay that long.

The poems I am assigned to read include part of Cole's Wordsworthian "Lament for the Forest" and the old chestnut "Woodman, Spare That Tree" (it does have an author, but I forget who). My neighbors in this segment are Harold Bloom,

Mr. Hollander, Thylias Moss (who, since she doesn't fly, has driven from Michigan), Robert Pinsky, and Roberta Whitehead. The second segment features James Merrill's superb renditions, at once plangent and feline, of Longfellow's "The Wreck of the Hesperus" and Poe's "Annabel Lee." Anthony Hecht and X. J. Kennedy, respectively, do beautifully with Longfellow's "The Jewish Cemetery at Newport" and Holmes's "The Wonderful One-Hoss Shay." Cynthia Ozick is assigned some fairly juicy Whitman passages (do I recall "scented herbiage of my breast"?) and Poe's "Conqueror Worm," but what I remember best is a poem by Christopher Cranch (one of the numerous poets the anthology rescues from oblivion) in the voice of an elderly tabby cat. Ozick duly read, her eyes demurely cast down, "I am a very old pussy. . . ."

November 1. Under the auspices of Poets' House the four hundredth birthday of George Herbert is marked by a reading down at New York University. Amy Clampitt, Henri Cole, Jane Cooper, Alfred Corn, and Stanley Kunitz each talk about Herbert and read a few poems, while almost everyone in the audience seems to be following along in one or another of the many editions of Herbert now currently available (the most recent of these, Ecco Press's *The Essential Herbert*, edited by Anthony Hecht, came unglued almost as soon as I bought mine). Hale and tan at eighty-seven or so, Stanley Kunitz recalls that at Harvard in the 1920s J. Robert Oppenheimer was a big Herbert fan and particularly loved "The Collar," which Kunitz proceeds to read passionately. Alfred Corn's rendering of "Discipline" seems stagy and rhetorical by comparison. Jane Cooper's soft, limpid "The Flower" brings tears to my eyes. Heading uptown on the subway—we're neighbors, more or less, on the Upper West Side—Jane and I talk about memoirs, archives, letters, memories. Six Degrees of Separation department: when Jane was growing up in Jacksonville, Florida, her father was the doctor (or was it lawyer?) of the family of Hellen Ingram, who became the mother of Jane's contemporary, James Merrill.

November 15. At the Greenwich House Music School, on Barrow Street in the Village, under the auspices of *Hellas,* a little magazine based in Philadelphia, I read from my work.

The audience is tiny but friendly: a couple of Rutgers colleagues and the essayist and critic Phillip Lopate sit near the front. Having recently given readings in Norfolk, Virginia, and then Dallas, I reflect that there's something to be said for personally knowing almost every soul in your audience.

November 16. At the National Arts Club, a landmark mansion in Gramercy Park that originally belonged to Samuel Tilden (best remembered for having almost beaten Rutherford B. Hayes in the 1876 presidential election), Thom Gunn is awarded the Lenore Marshall Prize, ten thousand dollars worth of goodwill now administered by the *Nation* magazine, whose editor, Victor Navasky, speaks first. He is followed by Robert Pinsky, head of the panel of three judges who awarded Gunn the prize. After Pinsky, whom I last saw at the Y on October 24, when he read Joel Barlow's "To a Raven in Russia," Gunn reads briefly from his wonderful book *The Man with Night Sweats,* ending with the poem about recognizing a former lover in the street accompanied by the young man's adopted child. Chat with Gunn: he has just seen *Perestroika* and compares Roy Cohn to Falstaff. With Pinsky: he's translating the *Inferno* and (shades of Milton?) his daughter is doing the notes to the edition. Dana Gioia, his head presumably still full of Longfellow from the Poets' Corner ceremony, suddenly appears and tells us that the best notes on Dante are by . . . you guessed it, Henry Wadsworth himself.

November 29. Déjà vu all over again at the Pierpont Morgan Library, a palace on 36th Street. Daniel Hoffman, under the auspices of the Academy of American Poets, reads from his work at what must be one of the only surviving black-tie literary events. Well, not all black-tie: the men are instructed to wear "black tie or business attire." So many of the women wear black that I'm reminded of the Ascot scene in *My Fair Lady.* Drifting through the exhibits before the reading begins, I see Arthur Schlesinger Jr. and his much taller wife, and for a second think I'm seeing Mr. and Mrs. Henry Kissinger.

And who should introduce Hoffman but Dana Gioia? From Longfellow to Hoffman. . . . Genially, Gioia confesses the difficulty of summing up as protean a writer as Hoffman; he's had to have recourse to the *sortes Vergilianae* method, flipping through Hoffman's *Collected Poems* and coming upon, now a taut lyric about Provence, now a poem starting "In the days of Rin Tin Tin."

December 1. After teaching my Columbia class, I whisk across the river to Newark, New Jersey, where the AIDS awareness stamp is being unveiled at the downtown post office at a ceremony where I've been asked to read from a book of AIDS poems I edited a couple of years ago. But the mikes aren't working, the audience is restless, and this occasion is, as I had suspected, one of official uplift and celebration—no time for dark broodings on mortality. Never before have I edited poems in the process of reading them, but there's always a first time. In a few minutes it's all over, and I have time to do some holiday shopping in Herald Square on the way back home to rest before the evening, when I'm scheduled to introduce three out-of-town poets for the Poetry Society of America.

Back down at the National Arts Club, the Sculpture Court is now pitch black in observance of the AIDS anti-holiday December first has become: the Day without Art. (The reading isn't to be in the Sculpture Court, however, but in the basement.) I'm to introduce three poets grouped together under some such rubric as "Blood and Soil." Hmmm. One of the three, Jared Carter, is ill and can't leave Indiana, so the readers are Gloria Vando and Carl Phillips. They are an oddly assorted pair: she a Puerto Rican–American whose simple poems mostly seem to chronicle family history; he an African American and ex–graduate student of classical philology whose strikingly elegant poems are aloof, erotic, and not in any obvious way "about" anything. Awarding Phillips a prize a few years ago, I had the privilege and pleasure of judging his manuscript *In the Blood* blind and therefore of having to infer—or, better, ignore—his gender, race, sexuality, and all the rest of the checklist we are now routinely supposed to apply to anything we read.

December 13. At the 92d Street Y James Merrill reads from his recently published memoir, *A Different Person*. I have heard Merrill read many times, never less than beautifully—till tonight. He has a cold and sore throat, his voice wavers away from the microphone, and he seems to have trouble keeping his place, perhaps because in prose the lines are longer. Or it could simply be that many of his poems he knows by heart—like "The Country of a Thousand Years of Peace," which he recites near the end of the evening. The audience chuckles at the worldly humor of passages from the memoir, but I sense a puzzlement in the air (and no wonder) when Merrill reads from the final book of *Sandover, Scripts for the Pageant,* a ballade about the fact that Maria was really Plato all along.

Merrill's introducer tonight isn't, for a change, a poet, but the novelist Allan Gurganus. Sparing us a cloying catalogue of Merrill's many honors, Gurganus speaks instead of the envy a child feels when he sees another, more skillful child draw—oh, an elephant—much better than his own. "That's *good!*" says the child in awe. "How rare it is, my friends," says Gurganus (and how unusual thus to address one's audience directly!), "how rare it is when the great man is also the good man."

December 15. Mark Rudman, my friend and neighbor, reads from his new book of essays, *Diverse Voices,* at the Nicholas Roerich Museum, a well-kept secret of a place only a few blocks from where I live, in a Beaux Arts building just off Riverside Drive on 107th Street. (Not that the paintings of Roerich deserve much fame—at best, they resemble Franz Marc on a terrible day. All in all, though, *vaut-le détour.*) Introduced by the Southern poet and novelist Charlie Smith, Mark reads from an essay on walking around the city, then excerpts from a book-length poem, *Rider,* about the Wandering Jew—or, depending on how you look at it, about Mark's late stepfather, Rembrandt's Polish Rider, motorcycles, Wyatt Earp's Jewishness. "Mark moves as we would move if we were fully awake," Charlie says in his introduction, which also refers to the "roughed-up Edens of city and desert." But Mark's long, loping lines seem to me, if anything, hypnotic, mesmerizing. And who in this city, as the winter closes in and we sidestep the huddled homeless, can bear to be fully awake?

December 16. The final literary event of my season is a luncheon sponsored by the U.S. Information Agency at which a group of visiting writers from abroad are to mingle with American writers, editors, and arts administrators. Once again, we're in the National Arts Club. I'd envisioned long tables with starched white cloths, name tags, place cards. In fact the occasion is informal—people are free to cluster, so of course they do, mostly with their own compatriots. Among mine are Edith Kurzweil, managing editor of *Partisan Review*, Eliot Figman of the arts organization Poets and Writers, the novelist and feminist Meredith Tax, and the poets John Ashbery, Gerald Stern, and Philip Levine.

I chat with a Moscow poet (good English) accompanied by his mother (good French); a Chinese poet who's staying out in Easthampton translating work by David Ignatow; an Egyptian novelist who quickly gets into a huddle with Meredith Tax about human rights abuses. Name tags do serve a purpose—I can't remember any of these people's names without them. But I do recall vividly a conversation over dessert with a woman in a beautiful red and green silk sari. Originally from India, she has gotten her Ph.D. degree in Australia, writing about Henry Vaughan. Now married to a Nigerian, she is living and teaching in Nigeria.

I mention the George Herbert celebration of earlier in the fall, and her face lights up. "But nobody in Nigeria wants to read Metaphysical poetry, so now I do postcolonial women's literature—African, Caribbean," she says. "You have to diversify."

Tangled Web Sites

In his 1930 address titled "Education by Poetry," Robert Frost raises some issues that have acquired added urgency over the past half-century. I am thinking in particular of a passage that lends itself to being read as a humanist exhortation toward the better understanding of poetry but that is really concerned with the way we think. Frost writes:

> unless you are at home in the metaphor, unless you have had your proper poetical education in the metaphor, you are not safe anywhere. Because you are not at ease with figurative values: you don't know the metaphor in its strength and its weakness. You don't know how far you may expect to ride it and when it may break down with you. You are not safe in science; you are not safe in history.

The idea of metaphors as risky things isn't peculiar to Frost. One example that comes to mind (and there are undoubtedly many more lurking out of my reach) is from Kathleen Norris's recent book *The Cloister Walk*. In her account of her experiences as a Benedictine oblate, Norris refers to

> our fear of metaphor . . . our denial of whatever is unpleasant or uncontrollable. As a writer, I know how unpleasant, even scary, metaphor can be. It doesn't surprise me that people try to control it in whatever way they can.

Norris has a point. Still, I'd maintain that reality is even scarier than metaphor—is in fact the reason scary metaphors exist in

---

From *New England Review* (spring 1998).

the first place. If anything, metaphor can be lullingly euphe-
mistic, as in phrases like "the next generation of missiles."
That such euphemisms are insidious doesn't make them fright-
ening, exactly; it makes them unsafe, or rather makes us un-
safe when we unthinkingly rely on them. Such reliance is what
Frost has in mind in "Education by Poetry" in the luminous
phrase I italicize in the following passage. Giving an example
of the power of metaphors, Frost observes that the metaphor
of evolution

> has interested us in our time and *has done all our thinking for
> us.* . . . I know the metaphor will break down at some point, but
> it has not failed everywhere. It is a very brilliant metaphor, I
> acknowledge, though I myself get too tired of the kind of essay
> that talks about the evolution of candy, we will say, or the evolu-
> tion of elevators—the evolution of this, that, and the other.

Frost's perception that popular metaphors infiltrate our lan-
guage and hence also our thoughts, thus coming to do our
thinking for us, is more suggestive than either Norris's rather
conventionally poetic defense of the untrammeled power of
metaphors or the familiar, dismissive phrase from George Or-
well's "Politics and the English Language," *dead metaphors.*
(Dare one suggest that this phrase has itself become a dead
metaphor?) Like Frost before him, Orwell disapproves of the
laziness and passivity of the run of language users. But it
doesn't seem so certain that metaphors really can be said to die.
They do seem to tire: a certain staleness of expression or a
prefabricated shortcut quality are among the depressingly fa-
miliar results. But a subtler and more interesting problem than
the graying of metaphors is their astonishing persistence and
vigor once they take root—an energy so palpable we naturally
assume that (in Frost's wonderful phrase) we can ride them
forever.

Is this metaphoric vigor a good thing? I don't know. But I
do know that, just as Frost was evidently growing tired, in
1930, of the evolution metaphor, I have recently begun to feel
pressured by the leading metaphor of our own day. (It was this
sense of pressure that reminded me of Frost's essay, not the

other way around.) The nature of the current metaphor is indicated by my title, and I'll get to it in just a moment; but I want to return first to Frost's observations about the long life of the metaphor of evolution.

Granted that were Frost around today, he would still—assuming he read the newspapers and watched television—encounter the evolution metaphor in phrases like "the next generation of" products ranging from computers to drugs for cancer. (I say *products* advisedly. Both of the examples Frost adduces in his essay, candy and elevators, are machine-made rather than organic, which may be part of why he's weary of references to them as having evolved like growing things.) But, in the seventy years since "Education by Poetry" was first published, the metaphor of evolution has indeed broken down, just as Frost predicted it would. Or, if not broken down, come to seem a bit passé, its power to account for our experience having become markedly attenuated.

The reason is clear enough. We no longer believe that on the whole things are progressing, developing, improving, moving toward fulfillment. For as long as I can remember the *New Yorker*'s caption "Onward and Upward with the Arts" has had an ironic ring. Despite the proponents of the Gaia hypothesis, we are much less likely these days to hear the kind of talk Frost vaguely reports on in "Education by Poetry": "somebody . . . said that the whole universe, the whole of everything, as like unto a growing thing." As we approach the millennium, we may or may not feel a part of something alive and growing. My own sense is that many people feel, or talk as if they feel, not more but less alive. What we indisputably do feel, however, is *connected,* wired to a network. The metaphor of evolution has given way to the metaphor of the web.

The phrases *World Wide Web* and *web site,* not to mention the term *Internet,* have gradually become household words. This first came home to me in the fall of 1996, when I encountered the following usages in the space of a week or two and experienced the sensation of a person who, having learned a new word, suddenly sees it everywhere. Old or new, dangerous or benign, this metaphor was definitely ubiquitous.

- The cover story of the November 1996 issue of the children's magazine *3–2–1 Contact* reads "Web Sites—Amazing Spider Hangouts."
- Describing the development of BIT NET, an early computer network, a professor reminisces: "To enter BIT NET, a new school just had to buy a pair of modems and a phone line to the previous school, like an ungoverned spider plant growing."
- Reviewing a book entitled *The Prehistory of Mind*, Jerry Fodor writes in the *London Review of Books* (Nov. 28, 1996): "What's your favorite metaphor for minds? If you're an empiricist, or an associationist, or a connectionist, you probably favor webs, networks, switchboards."

Even before all these instances, I'd been struck by a passage in Steven Pinker's introduction to his 1994 study *The Language Instinct:*

> some cognitive scientists have described language as a psychological faculty, a mental organ, a neural system, and a computational module. But I prefer the admittedly quaint term "instinct." It conveys the idea that people know how to talk in more or less the same sense that spiders know how to spin webs. Web-spinning was not invented by some unsung spider genius and does not depend on having the right education or on having an aptitude for architecture or the construction trades. Rather, spiders spin spider webs because they have spider brains, which give them the urge to spin and the competence to succeed.

This recurrent metaphor calls for a bit of disentangling, for it suggests several things at once. The figure is versatile: it can evoke spinning or weaving; spider or human activity; instinct or accomplishment; the look and behavior of a certain plant or what James Merrill, in *Mirabell: Books of Number,* calls "an entire life-fabric / woven of language." No wonder a trope so protean and adaptable has taken hold (or evolved) so well.

Popular as it is these days, the web complex is, of course, hardly new. In fact, it's easy to regard the explosion of web metaphors in tandem with the technological developments of the last ten years or so as merely the latest form taken by a venerable set of linked ideas. Evolution is really a newcomer by comparison. But to postmodern sensibilities evolution now feels a little dated, while webs, having once been associated with Athena or Penelope or Arachne, remain as tenacious as ever.

Nor has the essential meaning of the web metaphor changed all that much—at least in one of its essential meanings. Images of spinning and weaving, and hence of networks and reticulations in general, tend from very early on in the poetic tradition (that is, Homer) to connote communication and connection. Hence, by implication and extension they come to suggest not merely the products of spinning and weaving (thread, yarn, textiles) but arts related to language. Not only is early Greek poetry replete with images of both spinning and weaving: spinning and weaving are themselves among the earliest figures for poetic activity, as well as being associated with the machinations of fate or the Fates. One's destiny is spun, measured, cut, sometimes by—vaguely—the gods but often more specifically by female powers whose expertise naturally lies in the field of domestic handicrafts: they spin, measure, and cut the thread. The role of poetry is in part to record the results of these fateful activities.

At the risk of sounding like John Hollander's

> diachronic bore . . . [who] insists that a *text* is something woven, because it descends etymologically from the Latin for *web,* something woven, the rhetorician Quintilian pointing out that it was a trope when applied to something woven out of language . . .

let me point out that the connection between web-weaving and words does indeed surface in the kinship between *text* and *textile*. Alfred Corn—diachronically, perhaps, but not tediously—points out in his recent prosody manual *The Poem's Heartbeat* that

> the word "line" comes from the Latin *linea,* itself derived from the word for a thread of linen. We can look at the lines of poetry as slender compositional units forming a weave like that

of a textile. Indeed, the word "text" has the same origin as the word "textile." It isn't difficult to compare the compositional process to weaving, where thread moves from left to right, reaches the margin of the text, then shuttles back to begin the next unit.

But if the web image is so old, why does it deserve any special attention right now? In pondering it, I recognize that I have two opposing motives: reassurance and anxiety.

If there's nothing new under the sun, then the perennial trope of spinning and weaving is simply part of our cultural inheritance, in which case it merits a closer look, if only to refresh our memories. After all, it wouldn't take much doing to compile a little anthology of poetic passages ranging from Homer and Hesiod to Thom Gunn that work variations on the web theme. Such a gathering would reassure: see, the web image has been with us all along! But it might also show that all along the image has been a fraught one, rich with multiple meanings but also colored by coercion, its implications blurry.

The status of the weaver is surely ambiguous as early as Ovid's celebrated version of the story of Arachne's metamorphosis. Arachne begins as a young woman but is violently transformed into something less—or is it something more? Athena's motive in effecting the transformation is said to be pity; after all, Arachne is in the process of committing suicide by hanging herself when the goddess takes over. But Athena's act feels more like parody than charity, since, in becoming a spider, Arachne is being eternally imprisoned in the toils of her own excellence as a weaver.

Recall Pinker's point about what it takes to spin a web:

> Web-spinning was not invented by some unsung spider genius and does not depend on having the right education or on having an aptitude for architecture or the construction trades.

What was a celebrated accomplishment in Arachne the young woman has been demoted to the merely instinctive status of a spider's sole business; the very spinning that was a source of hubris has come to be a condign punishment.

The ambiguity of Arachne's metamorphosis finds more recent equivalents in various transformed or hybrid creatures who seem, like her, both more and less than human. I'm thinking of the ant collective visited by Wart in *The Sword and the Stone*, a world of terrifying regimentation and of unquestionably advanced communication; though T. H. White doesn't use the word, the ants are all plugged into a central network. In the collective the medium is the message; where commands are constantly broadcast, privacy is seen as wrong.

I'm also thinking of the Borg in the contemporary *Star Trek* fantasies. The uncanny, uncomfortable-looking, and sinister nature of these hybrid beings—part human, part insect, part machine, and all centrally controlled—is in keeping with Ovid's depiction of violently enforced metamorphosis. The Borg (note the collective noun) not only control superior technology; they are modules in that technology. Jerry Fodor's "webs, networks, switchboards" phrase is eerily close to the central core into which the Borg are all plugged, and we would do well to attend to their repeated warning: "Resistance is futile."

We have moved away from the image of a web. But it would be truer to say that if, as Frost reminds us, we can ride metaphors, the figure seems to have carried us to a strange place. Just how uncanny and incoherent the implications of the web metaphor have become was dramatized—only a few months after my initial intimation of proliferating webs—in March 1997, by the Heaven's Gate cult suicides, or rather by the media's reaction to that bizarre development. Much of the media response focused not on psychology, theology, or history but on the role of technology, since the Internet had been instrumental in spreading the cult's ideas. The question was posed in a number of ways whether the group's vision could ultimately be separated from the world of the Web. Was the Web merely a vehicle, or was it somehow actually responsible for the shocking fact of the group's suicide? In an article in the *New York Times*'s "News of the Week in Review" section (Mar. 30, 1997) that ruminates on this issue, the author seems unable to resist the lure of a whole host of images derived from technology.

As in the never-ending debates about television and violence, raised now to a new hyperactive plane, the question is this: Is the Internet a source of cultural sickness or just its reflection? As with television, cause and effect cannot be so easily untwisted . . . The effect is nonlinear, like the reverberative howl arising from a microphone held too close to a loudspeaker.

On the Net everyone can reach out and touch at random, in a way that's somewhat different from blindly dialing digits on a telephone pad. The Internet is the most efficient incubator of ideas both ennobling and debased. Each computer terminal is a shiny surface, reflecting not just things in the real world but things in the simulated reality of the Internet.

In the wilderness-of-mirrors [*sic*], a single string of mutant thoughts can be replicated over and over, distorted in the Internet funhouse until the result is impossible to untangle. Somehow the slick design of Web pages . . . adds credence to outlandish ideas.

No doubt these all are valid concerns. But, as Frost has taught me to see, the author of this article is letting a good many metaphors do his thinking for him. One encounters in these paragraphs a television, a microphone, a loudspeaker, a telephone, an incubator, a computer, a funhouse mirror, and, by implication, a strand of DNA. The generalizing phrase "things in the real world" pales by comparison with all this avidly evoked equipment: medium and message have begun to merge, not only for the hapless people who committed suicide but also for the journalist. Attempting to clarify the problem and enliven his prose, he rummages in the electronic supply store of his imagination, with the result that the digits, incubator, and so on are much more concrete and convincing than the vaguely labeled "ideas both ennobling and debased" or "real world." And if ideas and the world are less compelling to this journalist than a string of images drawn from technology, he is simply, perhaps, a citizen of his time. The real world, whatever that means, feels dull and slow, while the virtual world, with its jumpy energy, its unaccountable power to create new connections, is what's really news. Whatever the article's intention, the author is clearly more interested in the nonlinear effects of the Net than in whatever the alternative might be.

The article is short on specifics; the image of the Net has become a kind of shorthand for a whole host of technological developments in communication. As the reticulation grows more all-encompassing and powerful, it seems to become more mysterious, harder to classify and pin down. Source and reflection, cause and effect—in the virtual world these categories seem hardly to matter. The important, the mesmerizing, thing is the fact, not the purpose, of interconnection. In a half-jokey, faintly literary echo a Windows icon I saw the other day advised the user: "Just connect."

So the reassuring quality of the familiar is balanced by the undeniably creepy quality of the switchboard into which we're all being asked to plug ourselves. But the creepy also turns out to be the familiar, for the equivocal quality of web (as well as Web) imagery was surely there from the start. As we've seen, it turns up as early as the vengeful dehumanizing in the Arachne story or as recently as the reference to BIT NET growing "like an ungoverned spider plant." It appears in both what the *New York Times* reporter calls the spurious, pseudo-scientific authority exercised by "the slick design . . . of simulated reality" and in the classical scholar Laura Slatkin's observations about the celebrated ruse of Penelope in the *Odyssey*. Slatkin writes:

> As, in the literal act of weaving, material and design emerge simultaneously from a single process, so with Penelope the action of weaving and unweaving does not fashion a device but constitutes the device itself.

Penelope pretends to be weaving a shroud for her father-in-law, but she is really only weaving in order to be weaving (or, rather, in order to unravel what she has already woven and so to begin again), with the ulterior motive of holding the suitors at bay. Her "device" is not an artifact but a scheme. Penelope's fabled cleverness is thus indistinguishable from duplicity; her weaving is far more effective than words alone.

Webs, words, cleverness, deceit, medium, message, metaphor. Since most of us think in words, the very stuff of our thoughts is woven into the Web world, or vice versa. No wonder we let the figure do our thinking for us. If it is our nature to be ingenious, to develop ever faster machinery, perhaps it follows that it is also our nature to tailor language so that it mirrors more closely the world we are busy creating. Metaphor itself gets caught in a hall of mirrors as, tiny and garrulous, we spin industriously away at a giant net looped all over the globe. A real net? A virtual net? How could we extricate ourselves and begin to distinguish?

Part IV

Close to Home

A Poet's Life

An Interview with Rachel Hadas

Where else can we find sublimity but in the world in which we live?

As a whole, your oeuvre is preoccupied with the fundamental questions of mortality, metamorphosis, and rebirth. Biographically speaking, you seem to have risen from your own ashes (literally and metaphorically) more than a few times. In "The Dream of Divesting" (Mirrors of Astonishment), you wrote "When it's finally time to go away, / how much of myself shall I shed? / Happy the empty suitcase; / happier the empty head." How much of yourself have you shed thus far in your own life?

As far as rising from the ashes, I was tried for arson only once! But of course we do shed our successive selves in our lifelong trajectories, more like rockets than like phoenixes. Or do we? I live within a fifteen-minute walk of where I grew up. We spend summers in the house where I spent them as a child. The dining room table where I did my homework is now where my son does his homework. Continuity seems to be the theme. But continuity demands, if not rebirth, at least readjustment. Humanly speaking, I often fail to make the adjustment and so am hopelessly nostalgic for what cannot return. But art is where I am more courageous. Poetry enables me to face up to changes, if not to rebirths.

Another thought on the rebirth of the self is Oscar Wilde's wise comment, "It is impossible to change one's life. One merely wanders round and round the circle of one's personality." It strikes me for the first time that this may be a rather

From *Eclectic Literary Forum* 7, no. 1; interview conducted by Gloria Glickstein Brame.

infernal image. Yet one can also imagine the personality as a park through which one meanders, always getting home for supper. Certainly some personalities are more varied and spacious than others.

And what of the relationship of that parklike personality and art? Can one separate the artist from her art?

This is a point on which I am emphatically wishy-washy! If our selves keep changing, the whole matter surely becomes more complicated. Many of the literary-critical debates in our time can be defined as taking positions along a continuum, from "Yes, of course one should separate art and artist" to "No, no, artist and work are inseparable."

Personally, both as a reader and a writer, I am not concerned with the literal truth of a poem's contents. I know that any poem may float free of the facts of a life. But I do think that a temperamental link persists between the writer's style and his or her personality unless the writer utterly lacks any personal voice, in which case I'd soon lose interest in the work.

My Rutgers colleague David Hoddeson, describing his undergraduate years in the 1950s, uses a good image: the New Criticism (so-called) put a frame around the poem; author and a good deal else remained outside that frame. Eventually, the pristine text inside the frame came to seem too limited, too cut off from the world and the person from whom it took its being.

And yet how pristine was that text, really? The students had been reading lyric poetry all along; they already had a good deal of information about authors, literary periods, and so on. For students now reading big fat anthologies with double columns of print where poets are usually arranged in chronological order, the poet's "life," reduced to a short paragraph, is usually literally the introduction to the work, and naturally may seem more interesting, or at least more comprehensible, than the often difficult poems that follow the clear prose of the bio.

Such an arrangement clearly gets things backwards, but the severe separation of artist and work has problems too. So I think one negotiates back and forth, wishy-washily, fitting one's choice of response both to the nature of the work and the nature of the occasion. If you're writing a scholarly study of a writer, you will most likely connect the life and the art. If you know the writer, you can't help connecting them. But if you encounter a solitary poem in a magazine or anthology, then you can remain as ignorant as you like about the author's biography.

The Double Legacy *is a highly personal work—a series of contemplative essays on the deaths of two key figures in your life: your mother, Elizabeth Chamberlayne Hadas, and your friend, Charles Barber. In what ways did these two individuals shape or influence your poetic imagination?*

Well, my mother did the shaping. She was a wonderful mother, and my love of poetry—of all literature, really—has everything to do with the feast she set before me. Charlie came along too late in my life (I was almost forty-one when we met) to shape my imagination in that way, but he fed it and certainly thus influenced it, in the sense of inspiring poems (in fact he continues to do that) and enlarging my thinking in various ways.

If my mother was the principal person who introduced me to literature, Charlie, many years later, became with miraculous swiftness and remained for the two and a half years of our friendship my partner in a dialogue which in a sense continues even now, almost five years after his death.

*One of my favorite lines is in "On Dreams" (*Mirrors of Astonishment*), where you write, "FAX me your dream." We'll politely assume this isn't just a technological nightmare but expresses both some ineffable longing in you for a profound psychological immediacy with people you love and also a kind of despair at its impossibility. Do you think this impossible longing for perfect communion always existed and was tragically deepened by your adult experiences?*

You're right on the mark when you speak of my ineffable longing and despair. I think these twin feelings probably motivate and permeate much of my poetry. Are they simply part of my temperament, or do they result from my father's early death and my premature sense of the yoking of love and loss?

Are these feelings why I'm a poet, or has my poetry heightened them? Such questions suggest certain answers but cannot be answered with finality or certainty.

I would demur at your use of the word *tragically*. I've had a good many deaths in my life, but so does everyone, sooner or later. I have also had and still have a lot of love—a wonderful family and many friends—and work I adore and that absorbs me. Not everyone has that.

In the introduction to The Double Legacy *you say that you've omitted the small details of your daily life, largely because your everyday life was in abeyance during the period of your mother's and friend's illnesses and deaths. But your work, generally, is filled with small details—from the minute renderings of how it feels to be a nursing mother in* A Son from Sleep *to accepting your role as "Official Extricator of the Real from Everything That Isn't" (in "The Child Inquires Whether a Story Is Real," from* Living in Time*). Is the commonplace, for you, an aspect of the sublime?*

As Freud may have said, sometimes a cigar is only a cigar—and sometimes the commonplace stubbornly resists transformation. But in general, of course, where else can we find sublimity but in the world in which we live?

Wallace Stevens's "Sunday Morning" comes to mind here. "Divinity must live within herself: / Passions of rain, or moods in falling snow . . ."—as do James Merrill's words about Montale. Merrill observed that Montale's domestic imagery opened out into the uncanny: a hen or ladle or envelope "can take you straight from the kitchen garden to really inhuman depths." Much poetry, though of course not all, works some such alchemy. The sublime in the commonplace is a good touchstone for quality in poetry—not Ginsberg's "The asshole is holy" but Whitman, certainly. My poem "Little by Little," from the early 1980s, treats this theme, though I don't remember being aware of it at the time: "Let nothing be too big or small to say or see. . . ."

Mind you, the commonplace detail—the Band-aid on my burned hand, the cat yowling—is not necessarily sublime. I don't aim for sublimity in poems any more than I strain to avoid it. I distrust poems that seem to be obsessive litanies of detail. Nor do I warm to poems that sweep or swoop grandly over the terrain without focus.

Whatever my intentions have been, the poems I've written that deal with accessible, often everyday subjects by way of concrete detail have been among my most popular, though I'm certain that rhyme and meter have something to do with this response, too. Whereas earlier poems of mine that seem too abstract—no matter how carefully written—now bore me. Many of them apparently bored me years ago, since I didn't collect most of them into my books.

Passages and transitions are another major preoccupation in your work. Pass It On *is a structured meditation on transitions of all kinds including seasonal ones. Do you see your own life as passing in seasons? And if so, have you reached spring yet?*

Keats has a sonnet ("Four seasons fill the measure of the year") in which spring comes first. I'm forty-eight; wouldn't I be autumnal or something? Born in November, I adore autumn and tend to feel itchy, grubby, and distracted in the spring, which is part of what the phrase "spring fever" has always meant to me. A recent conversation with Richard Wilbur confirmed this sense of the term, though Dick didn't agree with my feelings about the season; I believe he's a spring man. His wife did, though.

There is also, thank God, the Indian summer provided by teaching. Every fall my autumn encounters the students' spring. I would like to maintain my autumn for a long time before winter. But spring? I feel as if that's over, if indeed it ever happened! My springs seem to be vicarious: my students', my son's.

Another way of looking at time in one's own life is as space. In the fall of 1988, when I turned forty and was away from home at an artists' colony, I had a vivid sense of myself as on an island, able to look forward and back. There was time ahead, but enough time had accumulated behind me so that I could see it. It was a peaceful feeling, this isolation. Both past and future were calm silver seas. I think periods like that recur in a life—I hope so.

In Living in Time, *you speak of a "moratorium" that occurs in the lives of many successful women artists—a time when their creative lives are at a standstill while the women attempt to decipher their personal identities (and destinies). You write that you felt your years in Greece were such a moratorium. Do you feel a life has only one such moratorium? Was this period of standstill a necessary part of your development as an artist?*

Let's give credit for the moratorium idea where it's due: to Carolyn Heilbrun's use (in *Writing a Woman's Life*), of Erik Erikson's concept, which Heilbrun extends, as Erikson did not, to women.

In the sense that the moratorium is a period of fertile inactivity, a sort of incubation, preceding a career, I'd say that once the career takes shape, the moratorium as such does not recur. But of course there are periods of latency, or blockage or exhaustion or just pause, between phases of any creative career. With luck, though, one phase or project often seems to give rise fortuitously to another. I know I'm not the only artist to have experienced this sense of reprieve or renewal.

Still, between the peaks are troughs. May Swenson has a wise iconographic poem, "HOW EVERYTHING HAPPENS (Based on a Study of the Wave)," on this subject. The troughs often feel desperately arid and flat while one's in them, but it's not so bad if there are other things cooking at the same time— thinking about a course, correcting papers, writing a book review, weeding the garden, or just reading. During such periods of pause the middle course—between waiting for inspiration to strike on the one hand and forcing oneself to crank out work on the other—can be difficult to steer. My husband, George Edwards, who is a composer, has always been for me a model of how to combine industry, patience, and an intuitive trust in one's own inscrutable rhythms.

Right now I'm not exactly in a moratorium, but, putting together my *New and Selected Poems* in time for my fiftieth birthday, I do find myself in a retrospective mood where my own work is concerned, rather than brimming with fresh inspiration. It's especially fortunate, then, that some god with a great sense of timing dropped a present in my lap a few months ago. *Helen,* the Euripides play I recently translated for the University of Pennsylvania Greek Tragedy series, is going to be staged here in New York later this spring, and I'm very excited about it.

The essays often weave intellectual tapestries whose threads are the thoughts and ideas of an astonishingly wide range of artists and scholars, living and dead. It is as if you are conducting a constant dialogue with these other voices. How important to the artistic process are these dialogues?

You know the answer: extremely important. Crucial. The idea of dialogue makes its way into the form of essays such as "The Farewells" (in *The Double Legacy*) and into the very title of my AIDS anthology, *Unending Dialogue: Voices from an AIDS Poetry Workshop.* The phrase *unending dialogue,* by the way, is from Kenneth Burke. (I'm not great at thinking, but I have a good memory for phrases. My husband has been known to call me an idiot savant.)

Friendships with poets—James Merrill and Alan Ansen, in particular—seem also to play a critical role in your aesthetic and emotional life. Are friendships among poets different from other friendships?

Friendship can be serendipitous in the same way as an unexpected project: someone will fall into one's life, apparently from heaven (though sometimes they turn out to come from some other place).

David Kalstone's book, *Becoming a Poet,* about the friendships between Marianne Moore and Elizabeth Bishop, and between Bishop and Robert Lowell, is a wonderfully subtle and tactful exploration of just how friendships between poets are different from other friendships. I think it was Bishop who wrote something about poets keeping warm by writing to each other.

Mark Rudman, for example, who lives across the street from me, now shows me more work than I show him; but there was a time when we'd shove things under one another's doors weekly. Nor is it only a matter of sharing the work. In my experience poets respect one another's struggle (a struggle invisible or uninteresting to most people) and are incalculably helpful to each other in ways they may not even know about at the time. A subordinate clause, an observation, a suggestion— something clicks.

Both from personal experience and from my knowledge of literary history, I think it's clear that poets nourish each other—what Bishop meant by keeping each other warm. They learn from one another's work and lives. Of course, they—may I say "we"?—are suspect as friends in that anything may go into a poem, including an argument, an unkind observation—anything. ("When they ask about inspiration," said Robert Frost, "I tell them it's mostly animus.") But once it's in the poem—if the poem lasts—the friendship, or that moment of it, however difficult, is encapsulated, preserved.

Merrill says in his memoir, *A Different Person,* that whereas human relations, like a picnic that may be rained out, are forever at the mercy of bad human weather—misunderstandings, contretemps, a bad mood—literature is not. I can think of plenty of people (many of them poets) I'm fond of with whom I nevertheless don't want to spend a lot of time. Well, poems aren't like that. They are always perfect companions. If you're not in the mood for them and leave for a while, they don't complain. Lyric poems are so deliciously self-contained, so free of the canine panting of narrative, which wants to tug you onward for a few more pages (another kind of pleasure).

I seem to have moved from talking about poets' friendships to considering poems themselves as friends. Fair enough. Every poet I know is aware of an uncomfortable pull between the gregarious and solitary sides of her or his nature. You love people but need to get away from them in order to write your poems, which are often about unrequited love, or like letters to absent friends, and so the spiral or cycle goes.

In light of the themes of metamorphosis and transition in your work, it seems natural that you would also be an avid translator of several languages. Other Worlds than This *contains highly original translations of an eclectic assortment of poets—from Tibullus and Seneca to Victor Hugo and several Symbolist poets and ending with translations of Greek poet Konstantine Karyotákis. Is the art of translation for you another way of changing yourself, even as you change the work of others?*

I love the double sense I have in translating of serendipity and surrender. Translating is also, among other things, a way of negotiating a dry passage: taxing one's verbal skills while pouring oneself into a formal vessel not of one's own choosing. Forcing myself to render ideas and feelings as skillfully as I can, I forget to worry about my own lack of inspiration.

Am I saying that whatever one thinks one is doing at the time, any project that seizes the imagination turns into another version of the self, another chapter in the ongoing oeuvre? Something like that.

I'm proud of my translations. Maybe I'll be remembered (if I am, which is a huge *if*) in the future as a gifted translator who also had a career as a poet.

What appeals to you most about translating the works of classic writers?

What's not to like? At the very least, one reads the text with fresh urgency. Or one may even be reading it for the first time. Either way, it exercises a pull. Some of Baudelaire's poems, which I translated in 1990 and 1991, when my friendship with Charlie was very intense, seemed to have been originally written about the relation between AIDS and eros. And Euripides' *Helen,* a magical play, is about female identity and, not coincidentally, survival, reinventions, rebirth. It's about a happy marriage.

In "The Cradle and the Bookcase" (Living in Time) you use personal essays and poems to explore your life as a reader—shifting points of view from scholar to artist, mother, wife, and daughter. Is reading as important to you now that you are in your forties as it was to you when you were a girl? Do you read for the same reasons now as then?

I read with less intensity and certainly less retention now than I once did. I read for different reasons, or for a greater variety of reasons, than when I was a child. But I think reading at any age satisfies a variety of needs and appetites. One reads for so many different kinds of pleasure, from escapism, vicarious thrills of all kinds, to information, aesthetic delight, narrative pull, amusement, entertainment—full circle. Furthermore, when various subliminal uses or purposes combine, and a nugget of text floats to the mind's surface, reading turns out to be not a pastime but a substance and a method. In a way, reading is not just food for thought; it is thought. John Hollander has said that writing is a more difficult form of reading.

As plenty of people have said, books are one of the great inventions; are more fun to take to bed or the beach than computers; are beloved by children. Alas, it is also manifestly true that the peace and quiet needed for reading as well as the function of reading as a source of information and recreation are both under siege.

As a teacher and a mother, what is your hope for future generations of readers?

As a teacher, I would stand on my head if it encouraged my students to read. I read to them, with them, we read aloud. Teaching at Rutgers gives me a chance to reread books that can never be worn out (like the *Iliad, Walden,* Jane Austen's novels) and a chance to try out in the classroom books that gave me a frisson when I heard them read aloud, like David Ferry's superb version of *Gilgamesh.*

Poetry brings things together—sometimes very unlikely things—and teaching gives one a chance to show how that works. This fall, teaching *Gilgamesh,* I had the courage for the first time to juxtapose part of one of Charlie Barber's poems with the ancient lines brought to life by Ferry. Whether it was the doomed Enkidu's dream of the House of the Dead or the AIDS sufferer dreaming of death as an office building in lower Manhattan, weren't the similarities greater than the differences, and didn't the language leap lightly over millennia? And, as a teacher, a mother, a whatever, I got to spread this feast out for others.

Poems and Dreams

Dreams and poems are engaged in some of the same tasks and use some of the same tools. Both, in my experience, somehow know and can convey unappealing truths to which the waking person, the person living her daily life in prose, seems to lack access. Or is it just courage that she lacks? I was writing poems foreshadowing the end of my first marriage long before I'd admitted to myself that it was ending. A dream informed me of my mother's fatal cancer a week or two before her diagnosis.

Both poetry and dreams often make lavish use of images; both often move laterally, erratically, by means of what I think of as lyric leaps. Both can be screamingly clear or hermetically difficult to construe. Both are mysterious in their provenance, seeming to come from deep within the self yet also reaching us as if from outside. Both can be zanily solipsistic yet can also command an impersonal kind of authority. It's not surprising, then, that for me, as for many poets, dreams are not only rich sources of imagery but something more. They feel like messages from another world, an intangible place that is nevertheless every bit as vivid and valid as the everyday world of waking reality.

As we all know, dreams often melt away, leaving, as Prospero put it, not a wrack behind. The medium I use for simultaneously fixing dreams in my memory and trying to make sense of them is poetry. Many of the dreams I succeed in recalling touch upon the same themes many of my poems do. One such theme is people I loved, have lost, and continue to love. Three

---

"Poems and Dreams" is from *Night Errands: How Poets Use Dreams*, edited by Roderick Townley, © 1998. Reprinted by permission of the University of Pittsburgh Press.

such poems follow, with a little commentary. One is about my friend Charles Barber; it was inspired by a dream several years after his death. The other two, about James Merrill, grew out of dreams within months of Merrill's death.

"Around Lake Erie and across the Hudson" recalls and examines one of those dreams that seem to happen just before one wakes up and begins the day. This day was a day I went to work, commuting as usual from Manhattan to my teaching job at Rutgers in Newark, riding west across the Hudson as the sun rose. It seemed important to get the real journey across the river, as well as the dream journey around Lake Erie, into the poem.

The dawn dream had a vividness, clarity, and above all a joy I wanted to capture. The spare format of quatrains helped me pare away irrelevancies and highlight details such as the haircut, the sweater, and the precise seating arrangements in the car, even if I wasn't sure what these details meant.

I did know why Lake Erie was in my dream. The *you* of this poem, Charlie Barber, is a beloved friend who had died some years previously but who in this remarkably happy and hopeful dream returns. (Even as I dreamed it, I understood that such a return was an impossibility, and that understanding too goes into the poem.) Charlie came from Cleveland, where his parents and sister still live. I've kept in touch with his family; but I've never been closer to Cleveland than the airport. Certainly I've never driven around Lake Erie, and I somehow doubt that the lake is as huge, sparkling, and blue as the white-capped, oceanlike expanse in my dream.

Why do we dream of our dear dead as and when we do? More than four years after Charlie's death, my grieving for him had lost its rawness. Was this dream a reminder of what I'd lost or a reassurance as to how much I'd kept by way of memory and sheer feeling? Coming at the start of a long day, it did indeed make me want to give thanks as I rode west into New Jersey and the sun rose behind me: thanks for morning light, for consciousness, for life itself, of which mourning our dead is a part. Crossing the river came, as I worked on the poem, to seem less like a "true" detail than like part of the dream itself. Wasn't the Hudson really a version of the mythological river that separates sleep from waking, or the dead from the living? Both dreams and poems lend themselves to such deeper meanings, for both are worlds unto themselves, with their own mysterious laws.

Around Lake Erie and across the Hudson

A rotten week, affections
grating against the grain.
I wake up, eyes beclouded
by the gift of a dream.

First an anxious journey,
directions barely heard,
lockers, crowds, and tunnels,
the destination blurred . . .

But then, ah! Calm perspective.
As if I were awake,
we three are slowly driving
around and around the lake.

You at the wheel, your sister
in front along with me.
Blue water, little whitecaps.
Brilliant October day.

You have a brand new haircut.
Your sweater's white and red.
Such vivid preparations—
as if life lay ahead.

Deliberately driving,
you cannot turn to me.
But conversation ripples
among us easily,

sister, friend, and brother
catching up: what's new?
And underneath the chitchat lie
two things we three know.

One, that we are joyful,
and two, this isn't real
miraculously coexist:
a miracle that still

tinges both past and future
with possibility,
although this outing never was
and will not ever be.

The shining lake, our chatter—
I carry them to work.
On New Jersey Transit
west out of New York

the rising sun behind the train
gilds pylons, bridge, gas tanks.
A purple cloud. A single gull.
I find I'm giving thanks.

I've dreamed about James Merrill many times, both during the twenty-six years of our friendship and since his death. In the two poems that follow, Merrill's death makes itself felt obliquely. These poems aren't joyful if fantastical reunions, like "Around Lake Erie and across the Hudson." Rather, they both in different ways explore the way a person no longer living is nevertheless central—a presence, a motivation.

In "May" Merrill is present, but just barely; he hurries away as if for an important appointment, the nature of which is all too easy to imagine. In "Tea and a Dream" he is absent— "gone"—but in a sense all the more present. Both dreams feature public structures—a lobby, an elevator—and are populated by groups of people, specifically, in "Tea and a Dream," by poets. This sense of a group is absolutely true to the feeling after Merrill's death of a circle of grieving friends, many of whom were poets. No one person could claim to have been central to Jimmy's life, but then no one had to bear the loss alone either. As Richard Kenney wrote to me at the time, "We all collapse a little; may it be toward each other."

And toward Merrill too. For both these poems, like "Around Lake Erie," use the second person, lyric poetry's distinctive way of turning toward the person to whom the poet speaks. The intimacy of apostrophe is in no way invalidated by the death of the person addressed.

Elizabeth Bishop dreamed at least once about George Herbert. Robert Frost did appear to me in a dream years ago—

was it because as a child I'd met the famous old man? I don't dream, or haven't yet, of Sappho or Keats, Dickinson or Whitman. But I feel very fortunate that the poet who was my dear friend continues to be a living presence in my dreams.

May

The latest dream: a lofty hotel lobby,
honeycombed with entrances and exits.
Feeling weak, I find a corner, lean
against the pale gold alabaster wall,
and feel its coolness seep into my shoulders.
Suddenly you appear and hurry past me
on your way out. An open door, a car
waiting . . . I summon all my strength to say
before you vanish just how much I loved you.
I think you hear. You smile and then are gone.
The lobby like a hive, the steady stream
of transients moving in, out, up, and down;
empty and crowded world. Again alone,
I lean against the coolness of the stone.

Tea and a Dream

One eye open, on its little island
in the hotel moat, a green lagoon,
an alligator loiters. Four o'clock:
tea in the lobby with my hungry son.
Darjeeling, scones, meringues; but you are gone.
Pennies tossed into the fountain splash.
What do we wish for? Hush.

It is too late for thanks.
Repayment, rather—in what mortal coin?
You blow toward us in the soft Gulf breeze,
you shine on us in fitful springtime sun,
dismembered into myriad legacies,
scattered among the elements. You're gone,
an absence palpitating in my dream.

A black glass elevator,
sliding down the outside of a building,
shudders to a halt on the ground floor.
The passengers, all poets, getting out,

look at one another. It is dawn.
Has there been a party? You are gone.
Through avenues still silent we move off

in different directions
toward separate obligations
that await us—families, jobs, and time,
a lifetime's sum of days
on this strange foundation. You are gone.
The black box, emptied of its cargo, light,
rides again to a Parnassian height.

The Old Address Book, the New
Address Book, and the Bird Book

"Epameroi," wrote Pindar in his Eighth Pythian Ode—his Doric version of "ephemeroi," or ephemeral things. In Lattimore's translation:

> We are things of a day. What are we? What are we not?
> The shadow of a dream is man, no more.

And the street cry of newspaper vendors in Athens is—or at least it was twenty years ago—"Ephemerides, ephemerides!" One could render this *newspapers* or *ephemera*—probably *dailies* captures both senses. Or *journals.*

My mother, one of the most literate people I ever knew, died four years ago this spring. She kept no journals, which may be one reason I find myself so reluctant to throw away her old address book, presumably the last in a series. I can't even bring myself to throw away my own used-up one, even though the binding has come undone, the pages are almost all filled up, and I've already bought myself a pristine new address book.

Undeniably, address books do from time to time need to be not merely updated but replaced. Friendships wither (oh, why did I write down that name of all names in ink?). People move away and lose touch. New people appear, of course. Finally, people die. Whereupon I see that my mother's practice was to draw a firm diagonal through the whole entry, name, address, and all. This book in my hand offers plenty of such crossings

---

From *New England Review* (1997).

out. I, however, seem to feel the urge to annotate—to add, not subtract. I scribble the death date in the margin, one final bit of information embellishing the name. Thus, as my book fills up, it also takes on a pseudo-narrative flavor, at least a sense of closure.

But today, as if instead of the middle of summer it were New Year's Eve, resolutions hover around the replacement I've bought for my old address book. A stern inner voice intones: Write fewer names down. Save . . . save what? Space, ink, paper, energy, affection? Against the coming hibernation, the end of all new addresses, don't accumulate; cut back! Is that the idea? Something about the virgin address book confronting me certainly does stimulate a perverse taste for whiteness—an impulse, however fleeting, to wean myself, to just stop meeting people, keeping in touch with people, and above all annotating life in terms of name, place, number—to stop transforming people into paper.

As if by not writing down anything new I think I can avoid the final mordant postscript that awaits every entry, including my own.

My mother's old address book isn't the only volume she has left in lieu of a journal. Her well-worn copy of Roger Tory Peterson's *Field Guide to the Birds* offers marginalia of a much more cheerful nature than her diagonal lines or my obituary scribbles. Her practice was to look a bird up in the book and then use the book to note, sometimes very precisely, when and where she saw the bird. Thus, under Brown Creeper she has written "Riverside Dr. and Central Pk., April 1967." Mourning Dove: "1978, Danville-Peacham Road." And an iambic pentameter line that Frost might have written, following the date 5/31/82: "Belted Kingfisher flying down the brook."

The bird book and the address book are alike in being journals of a sort—the economic, Line-a-Day kind. Each in its own way, they both streamline information, as for an annal or an almanac. Gaps remain to be filled in, but the essentials of the record are there—essentials both faithful and limited because of their factual nature. Both Peterson and my mother, as writers, give a sense of immediacy, of the truth of an experience. Peterson's meticulous transcriptions of bird calls, for example, always seem true to what he has heard, not what others have written. This is a guess of mine; but, with my mother's book, I don't have to guess. If she saw a bird, she recorded it. Her copy—my copy, now—of Peterson is also full of dated lists of birds seen on a given summer, another form of annal.

What's left out is all those things I, as a writer, seem to concentrate on: not what bird or when but how it felt to see it; not which summer but essence of summer. Not so-and-so's name but what lunch with her was like or why the friendship petered out. The backdrop, then, but not only that. Was that birdwalk on a crisp morning or a hot afternoon? What mood was she in when she saw that scarlet tanager? Why was she in the country on May 31—did she get a ride up with Aggie and Freddie to put in the garden on a Memorial Day weekend? I wanted to know both more than she tells me and less—a matter of genre or generations or just two temperaments.

Exactness takes many forms, of course. Handbooks like Peterson's do not go out of date (though they may wear out) for the same reason that birdcalls can be accurately transcribed and predicted year after year. Fauna and flora obey perennial laws; what yearly vanishes and dies seems hardly to change, so reliably does each new season replace parents with offspring that, to human eyes at least, are identical. Thus Woody, the generic woodchuck that visits our garden every summer; thus what my father called Joe the chipmunk. No doubt to say this is to be intolerably species-ist. Woody may think we're new people every summer; or we may just be generically indistinguishable to him.

Nature stays the same, people change? That's too simple; people change nature and also change themselves—one reason we need to change address books. What does seem true is that, humanity being saturated in language and story, everything associated with people has a history, or histories. Jewelry, mirrors, shoes, cups—everything human has its narrative. "The house itself, if it had a voice, could speak," says the Watchman in Aeschylus' *Agamemnon*. But books alone (including notebooks, address books, bird books) not only contain but constitute narratives. Nothing else people leave behind is as lavishly inscribed as a book they have written in. I treasure the handwriting, the intimations of a summer, the faintly remembered name of a person my mother knew. I note what I know and don't know of what she has set down. I take my place as the next (though far more ignorant) birdwatcher. I decide to hold onto her address book and my old one and to start writing in my new one. Ephemeral creatures, we accumulate ephemera.

The Well

For years my family spent its summers in a kind of lavish squalor. Squalid lavishness might describe it better—a sloppy extravagance in which everything important was in generous supply. Time, weather, the size of the sky, the succulence of dreams—these concocted a dense humidity to paddle in. In the thick air of Julys and Augusts, all kinds of curious intricacies flourished. Leisure, memory, arguments, reconciliations, the next installment of friendship, a childhood—these were our daily fare.

All we needed was irrigation, for the only scanty element in this welter was water. We'd never been confident of the depth of our shallow well; indeed, late one August, at the end of a damp and cool and guest-crammed summer, the well had actually gone dry. That happened to be the fall we had planned to spend in the country, and spend it we did, with trowel and toilet paper ready on the porch table for trips to the pinewoods. The next spring the well, as they say, came back, but we'd finally learned to suspect that one day it would dry up for good.

So, almost twenty years after that fall of chilly excursions, after years of nervous hoarding and infrequent flushing and rare bathing, this turned out to be The Summer We Put in a Well. Not that we'd planned to do it this year rather than another. Rather, accumulated pressures seemed to ripen. It was a chore, a task left over from my mother's generation, an obligation, a bill come due. Simply something it was high time to do and get it over with.

The local dowser duly came and made a precise prediction: exactly here, 136 feet down, you'll get twelve gallons a minute.

From *Threepenny Review* (winter 1999).

Proved wrong when the drillers went to work (it was more than 300 feet and less than three gallons a minute), he responded that the drillers had *missed the vein.* Whereupon the tetchy voice of Richard III incongruously popped into my head, saying to an importunate noble, "I am not in the giving vein today." The silly doomed man insists on whatever he's asking for, and Richard snarls, "You trouble me. I am not in the vein."

This hidden vein of water: where and what was it? I pictured something spindly, sparkling, crystalline, elongated, frail, vertical—though, when the drillers had to resort to "hydrofrakking," it appeared these veins were horizontal. (Had they even nicked the elusive vein, we'd have had water bursting from the ground at twenty gallons a minute—a true Artesian well, not even a pump needed.) Even veinless we have, or think we have, more water than we've ever had before. Alas, years of careful conservation have sapped our invention: what to do with all this water? It's been the rainiest summer in years; the workers drilled in a downpour. Flush, then, and bathe, and bathe and flush again. Is that all? Shower? Washing machine? These appliances can wait another year or twenty.

This will last your time, the caretaker-cum-handyman said (he had worked for my father and mother and after that for my mother) when, a few years ago, we'd had a new foundation poured to arrest the house's venerable but worsening list. This appeared to be the order of business: my mother dies; the house, which has long tilted, tilts more and more precariously; fix the foundation, pour cement, shore up the cellar. Then (minor leaks in the roof having meanwhile been mended) it will be time to drill a well. Both well and foundation will presumably last our time, however long that is—something we do not know and do not want to know. Nor can we know it, lacking a dowser with his ready smile, his looseleaf notebook (bulging with well-documented testimonials of his success) tucked under his arm. Who would dowse the depth of their own life? Time, that column buried underground—its length, depth, thickness, overall dimensions, elusive location—is, despite the augurs with their magic wands and confident predictions, stubbornly unknowable and best unknown.